To John Thompson,
Best Wishes,
God Bless You,
Joe B Hu

Joe B. Hunt
Texas Ranger
campfire tales

TEXAS DEPARTMENT OF PUBLIC SAFETY
OFFICIAL IDENTIFICATION

JOE BURL HUNT
NAME

TITLE — TEXAS RANGER

SERVICE — TEXAS RANGERS

William E. Speir
DIRECTOR

In Memory of

My parents,
John C. Hunt and Willie Mae (Williams) Hunt

My father and mother-in-law,
Emil Goetz and Annie (Schacherl) Goetz

Dedicated to

My loving wife, Linda Hunt,
and granddaughters Brittny Hunt,
Taylor Hunt, and Rylie Hunt

Joe B. Hunt, retired Texas Ranger, from San Angelo, Texas was the honoree at the Annual Texas Ranger Association Foundation Ranger Reunion in Waco on June 14, 2013. Surrounded by his fellow Rangers and family members, Joe was recognized for his many years of service to the great State of Texas.

May GOD bless Joe Hunt and may GOD bless the Texas Rangers.

Foreword

I first met Joe Hunt in the mid-1970s when I was a young defense lawyer trying cases throughout West Texas. Even though at that point in my career I was always on the other side in court, I learned you could trust what he told you or testified to because he had that character trait most needed in criminal cases. Joe would "tell it like it was" or, as we say in Texas parlance, he wouldn't try to "doctor" the facts.

Later in 1979, when I took office as Lubbock's elected Criminal District Attorney, I came to rely greatly on the support that I received from the Texas Rangers. It was probably the best support team a DA could have—Captain Bob Werner, Joe Hunt, and Jackie Peoples from Texas Ranger Company "C." They were always there to help, particularly on tough homicide cases that needed better than average investigative work. These men were not arrogant or haughty but very thorough. They interacted well with all law enforcement agencies. They got the job done.

I would characterize these men as dedicated "Texas Law-men" in the truest sense of the word. I also liked working with the Rangers because they would always be candid about the evidence. If they thought we were on the wrong trail or if they thought I was after the wrong person, they wouldn't hesitate to tell me. They always had a good grasp of the facts and were effective witnesses.

To this day, I attribute a lot of my successes as DA, particularly with a long string of 99-year sentences for some really bad characters, to the work done by Joe Hunt and the Company "C" Rangers.

As I think back over many years and many careers, I recall one lighthearted episode with the Rangers. I thought I would use the occasion of writing this foreword to reminisce about it!

In late 1982, I was elected to the Texas Senate and served several terms. I had been campaigning for re-election. The Rangers had always invited me to their annual company meetings in the field. It was usually in a remote part of the 6666 Ranch and a great place to swap stories, wet your whistle, and downright saturate the evening with "shop talk." I had ended a very tough day of speeches and campaigning accompanied by my aide, Nelson Nease. We finally arrived on a rural stretch of road on the 4-6's. The Ranger Company and other lawmen were there in full force along with JJ Gibson, longtime foreman of the 6's. I believe his son Mike was also there. When we arrived I asked for a stiff drink, which I had always counted on at the Company meetings I attended in the bush. Seemed reasonable to me as we were in the middle of nowhere! We were met by a lot of sheepish looking faces by all of these "he men" who informed me that one of their Rangers had complained to Headquarters about the raucous effects of whiskey in the field. As a result, it was ordered that there could be no alcoholic beverages consumed on these retreats. I was shocked. As we sat around the campfire, I delivered the following memorial poem, fitting for the occasion:

> We were hot, tired and thirsty, eating West Texas dust
>   all day,
> Campaigning so far from cities, we could hardly find
>   our way.
>
> After all our electioneering and hand shakin',
> My ass was beat and really achin'.
>
> So we drove the back roads of Texas, my staffer and me,
> To hangout and drink whiskey with the lawmen of
>   Company "C."
>
> When we get there, in a place only God could find,
> They all looked so sheepish—they were in some kind of
>   bind.
>
> Under the stars with a campfire a-blazin',
> A fine drink of whiskey, my thirst was a-cravin'.
>
> They poured me a drink from a pitcher real nice,
> I thought to myself... don't drink whiskey with ice!
>
> I sat there in shock in the evenin' breeze,
> The mighty Texas Rangers were serving "ice teas."

I am proud to have been one of those fortunate Texans to have known and served with Ranger Joe B. Hunt.

John T. Montford
San Antonio, Texas
May 20, 2013

Contents

Texas Ranger
campfire tales

Introduction

When thinking of what I wanted to say in the introduction of this book, I considered many things, but one thought seemed to always get on out there a good ways in front of everything else. By this, I mean while there are many things I can say about my life, my family and my career; when it all comes together I realize the only way I had these good fortunes is for one good reason alone. I was simply, graciously blessed by our good Lord. Nothing in my life would have ever happened without His blessing, grace or mercy. I have been from the bottom of the valley to the top of the mountain and back several times. At this stage of my life, I know it is my Lord who has taken me on these journeys. I end up writing more on this at the end of my book, but I feel I must say now I realize my early childhood experiences, my testing of life, my adult years and my true discovery of the Lord in later life made me realize how truly blessed I am.

As I go about evaluating my life and career, I don't think there is any doubt the Lord has let me walk mostly on top of the mountain. He has shaken me a time or two and put me down there in that valley, but He is always gracious enough to help me back up. I know the Lord was with me several times during childhood and saved me from serious injury or death. The same can be said about my law enforcement career. The Lord has graced my family and my extended family in unbelievable ways. For these blessings, I give Him the praise and glory.

One of the Lord's greatest blessings was meeting a girl who grew up just down the street from me and marrying her in 1964. Linda didn't know she was marrying a man who would become a Texas lawman, but she has been a wonderful life partner and always managed to keep the home fires burning. I thank the Lord for her every day.

People have been after me for a good while now to write this book. These are stories you would hear sitting around a campfire with a bunch of old Rangers or Texas Highway Patrolmen. Most of us never had monetary riches, but we did have a very deep devotion to our comrades and a special understanding of one another. This devotion I believe, to some degree, will also be found in the DPS uniform services and your local law enforcement officers. Linda can tell you this, I will chase an old Ranger or Highway Patrolman down just to get him to stop and "swap" a few stories. I enjoy this storytelling time, I guess, as much as anything I do.

I want to acknowledge those who have helped on this book, especially my brother, Skipper Hunt, who is a retired DPS lieutenant, and my sister Carolyn Cornelius. Thanks to David and Pam Jones for all those computer lessons. Thank you, Vicki Draper, for putting the teacher's touch to the book. To my friend, Russell Smith, words can't express the appreciation I have for you. When it came time for the final edit, Skipper and I asked Candace Cooksey Fulton, whose father Bill Cooksey was a long-time law enforcement officer and educator we had known in our younger years, to give it one last going over. Finally, long-time friend, Jim Bean, designed the book cover and came up with the best title of the several that were suggested. I couldn't be more pleased. More thanks are due to all of those who brought up old stories they have heard or were a part of and shared with me. Some of those, I had truly forgotten and I loved reliving the memories and telling the stories again.

Everything in this book is factual and as true as I can remember. As with any Ranger story, one or two details might have been embellished just a little, but I will promise you none of the basic facts have been altered, even though a few of the small details may have been forgotten.

Again, I want to stress that this is not my book. This book belongs entirely to my Lord. Without Him, none of it would have made it this far. My intent for writing this book is to offer the reader some insights into the cases we worked in the Highway Patrol and the Rangers; to share our camaraderie as we all went about the business of enforcing the law; and then to let people see us as we are.

I don't have any intention at all to make money off of this book. I'm gonna pay for the first round and if any money is made, we will put those proceeds toward some foundation to further the Lord's work here on earth, to glorify Him and further His Kingdom. Hopefully, we will have enough left to buy another round for the Lord. Enjoy the book and please remember to praise your Lord and Savior every day.

The Beginning

"Joe, you ought to write a book." How many times have I heard someone say that? My response was usually "I will one of these days." They nearly always replied, "No, Joe, we're serious." Well, maybe they were right. I got to be a part of some very interesting events. They should be written down, but to tell my story, I can't just write about my law enforcement career, I want to touch on other parts of my life as well.

I like to think of myself as a native of San Angelo, Texas. Although my other siblings were born in San Angelo, I was born November 9, 1944, in Kermit, Winkler County, Texas. It was during World War II and my dad was a civilian carpenter assigned to the Army Air Corps base at Pyote. The nearest hospital to the base was in Kermit.

Right after the war, the family returned to San Angelo. I don't remember much about my early years. My dad, John C. Hunt, was a carpenter by trade. My mother, Willie Mae Williams Hunt, worked several jobs in those early years. My older sister, Carolyn, was born in December of 1941.

ANGELO'S HUCK FINNS — A raft on the Concho gives boys and girls a chance to enjoy a little spring fishing, but there is always a time to come home. Seated is Skipper Hunt, who is having time with his pup. Pat Horner, standing left, and Joe Hunt watch the shore. (Staff photo)

Huck Finns of San Angelo
Standing: Pat (Horner) McCrea, Joe Hunt
Sitting: Skipper Hunt with Tip
March 1957

6

After me, came John Wayne, or Skipper, who was born in February of 1952 and Jerry Don, who was born in March of 1956. Our family lived at the corner of 14ᵗʰ Street and Holcomb in San Angelo.

In the middle of my fourth-grade year, Dad moved the family to Midland, Texas. He built houses there for about a year. Then, Dad got a job as the Maintenance Director for the San Angelo Independent School District and we moved back to the Holcomb Street address in San Angelo in the middle of my fifth-grade year.

Before the start of my sixth-grade year, our family moved again, this time to a house furnished to us by the school district, near where the new Central High School was being constructed. We lived there through my seventh grade year. The house was located on the banks of the Concho River, which suited me just fine. My dog, Tip, and I spent many wonderful hours exploring places up and down the river.

Two things happened at the start of my seventh-grade year that remained fairly consistent in my life, at least they were constants until I retired from the Tom Green County Sheriff's Office in 2011.

The first of those two things was that I went to work. I had both morning and evening paper routes for the San Angelo Standard-Times. On days the weather allowed, I rode my bicycle early in the mornings from the house to the Standard-Times building, got and folded my papers there, then would ride to where my route happened to be. After delivering the morning paper, I would ride to school at Edison Junior High School. After school, I would ride to a location near my route—usually an abandoned service station located at the corner of Main Street and Harris Avenue on the east side of San Angelo—and the area manager would deliver my bundle of papers there. On bad weather days, Mother or Carolyn would drive me around my routes in a car. Bad weather included rain and snow, but not cold temperatures.

In addition to the paper routes, I had various part-time jobs and in the summers I worked with the school district. In high school, I finally got some real jobs that let me quit the paper delivery business.

The second thing to happen was I started paying installment loans. It seems like I have had an installment loan payment of some type most of my life, starting in the seventh grade when I bought a bicycle to deliver my papers on from Western Auto. The payments were $7 a month. I finally finished the last of my installment loan payments when I retired as Tom Green County Sheriff on March 31, 2011. When I retired, Linda and I were able to sell our house in San Angelo, pay off the ranch in Schleicher County, and move into the house we had built there.

With the exception of the one year, our family lived in Midland in the early 1950s, I lived in San Angelo until I left for service in the Texas National Guard. I attended public schools in San Angelo. I attended John Reagan and Santa Rita elementary schools, Thomas Edison Junior High and graduated from San Angelo Central High School in May of 1963. I started at San Angelo College in the fall of 1963. I dropped out of college to join the National Guard in January of 1964.

The Active Duty Army Life

I went to basic training at Fort Polk, La. then on to artillery training at Fort Sill, Okla.

I arrived at Fort Polk in early February of 1964, and was there for about nine weeks. The weather was pretty much miserable the whole time I was there, plus, when I arrived, they said several cases of spinal meningitis had been reported. Spinal meningitis is a highly contagious illness. So we would be on the lookout to know if we might be coming down with it, we were told some of the early symptoms to look for, such as a cough and red spots on your body.

This was my first time to be away from the "home nest" and I will have to say it took some serious adjustment. I remember arriving at the Fort Polk reception area on a bus that had picked us up at the train station in Leesville, La. Drill sergeants were there to greet us with lots of screaming and yelling. Nothing we did was right. I remember thinking, "What have I gotten myself into?"

Once the reception station activities and all the testing and orientations were completed, which took about a week, we were assigned a training company and moved to the barracks for that company. We finally began our training and things settled down somewhat.

On our third week of training we went to the rifle range to learn how to shoot the M-14 rifle. We spent the week there, sleeping at nights in our two-man pup tents. As usual, the weather was miserable. Well, as soon as we got to the rifle range that Monday, I began to feel bad. I began to cough and for four nights I could not lay down flat because of my cough.

We got back into the company headquarters at just about dark on Friday and by that time I was really sick. I also had red spots on my skin.

I went to the company headquarters office and went in. Pfc. Katz from New York City, N.Y., was the person on duty. I went up to his desk and told him I was really sick and thought I might have spinal meningitis. I opened my shirt and showed him the red spots on my body.

He immediately jumped out of his chair, backed up and started hollering at me to "get out" and "get out now." While he was hollering this, he was pointing toward the front entry door of the office. As I was on the way out the door, Katz told me to wait on the porch and he would call for an ambulance.

An ambulance came and took me to the hospital. Turns out, I had the measles. I stayed in the hospital until Monday then returned to my company to continue training.

The following week, I did qualify as "expert" with the M-14 rifle. That earned me a Saturday night pass for the weekend. A buddy, Leonard "Butch" Kelley, and I went to Leesville, ate in a restaurant, took in a movie and slept in a motel. That was sure a welcome relief from the Army barracks at Fort Polk.

After finishing training at Fort Polk, I got a two-week leave and then went to Fort Sill, Okla., for artillery training. There we learned how to shoot the 105mm towed howitzer cannon. Fort Sill was a lot more relaxed atmosphere than Fort Polk was. Once we got off duty in the afternoons, we were able to take in activities on post, such as movies, go to the PX where beer was served, and a few other things like that. Once in a great while, we were allowed evening passes to go into Lawton, Okla. I was at Fort Sill about 14 weeks. Fort Sill was a little closer to San Angelo, which allowed me to go home on weekend passes several times.

After completing my active duty training, I returned to San Angelo in the summer of 1964 to start my 5 plus years of reserve duty with National Guard. In December of that year Linda and I got married.

My State Service:
The Texas National Guard, the Texas Parks and Wildlife Department and the Texas Department of Public Safety

In March of 1965, I applied for and got a job with the Texas Parks and Wildlife Department working on a fish hatchery in Devine. We raised primarily black bass and channel catfish on this hatchery. There were thirteen hatcheries in the State of Texas at that time. Baby fish, or fingerlings as they were called, were given free of charge to citizens of Texas in order they could stock their ponds and small lakes. Excess fish were then released into public lakes and rivers. We delivered fish to several counties surrounding our hatchery.

While working at the fish hatchery, I applied to go to the Texas National Guard Officer Candidate School at Camp Mabry in Austin. In the spring of 1966, I tested for one of the openings and was accepted to start the OCS Academy, Class Number 10, in June of 1966.

OCS turned out to be one of the most demanding academies I ever attended. The classroom studies were very rigid with a high failure rate. The physical training, done in Army fatigues and heavy combat boots, was very hard and exhausting, but I came to appreciate it all the more once I started the DPS Law Enforcement Academy. The OCS Academy helped my conditioning for the DPS Academy greatly.

The OCS Academy started with a two-week summer camp at Camp Mabry. Then we had two days a month for 11 months, a full weekend each, that we attended classes and trained at Camp Mabry. We were to finish the academy with a two-week camp at Camp Mabry the following summer.

It was while I was working at the fish hatchery that I met two Texas Highway Patrolmen, Leonard Lewis and Mat Gullion. Both of these patrolmen were instrumental in convincing me I needed to become a Highway Patrolman for the Texas Department of Public Safety.

I applied for the DPS, was accepted, and on February 14, 1967 reported to the DPS Law Enforcement Academy in Austin to begin the 17-week training that would allow me to become a patrolman. Actually, the DPS Academy consisted of a basic 13 week course of study that all recruits were required to attend. This was called the Part One School. Then, depending on what service we were assigned, we continued on with specialized training in Part Two School. The Highway Patrol Service, License and Weight Service, and Capitol Security Service continued on for four more weeks. The Driver License Service and Motor Vehicle Inspection Service continued for two additional weeks after completion of the Part One School.

The training program consisted of intense classroom instruction and rigid physical training in both Part One and

Part Two Schools. I was 22 years old at the time I started the academy. Since I was already a member of the Texas National Guard and had been attending the National Guard OCS Academy, I was in pretty good physical shape.

I opted to apply for Driver License Service as I neared completion of the DPS Academy because that allowed me to finish my OCS Academy in the summer of 1967.

Our DPS Academy, "A" School, graduated in June of 1967. I was assigned to the Driver License Service, San Antonio. One week after graduation from the DPS Academy, I attended the final two-week summer camp at Camp Mabry in Austin that allowed me to graduate from the OCS Academy with a commission as second lieutenant in the National Guard.

My obligation to the Guard was a six-year enlistment, which terminated in February of 1970. At the conclusion of my

OCS Academy Class Number 10 Graduation
June 1967, Austin, TX

"A" School
Austin, TX
2/14 thru 5/26/67

DPS Academy "A" School Graduation
June 1967, Austin, TX

obligation, I resigned my commission as second lieutenant. I was honorably discharged from the National Guard in April of 1970.

I requested that the DPS transfer me from the Driver License Service to the Highway Patrol Service as soon as possible. My transfer was approved in May of 1970. I was sent back through the Highway Patrol Part Two School of the DPS Academy in Austin. At the completion of this school, I was commissioned as a Texas Highway Patrolman and assigned to the Odessa sergeant area.

I am thankful for the three years I served in the Driver License Service because it allowed me the opportunity to learn the organizational structure of the DPS, what was expected of an employee, and it also gave me plenty of opportunity to be in contact with the public. About every type of contact you can imagine comes through a licensing office, from pleasant, satisfied people to those who are not satisfied at all and are pretty angry and upset. These contacts, day in and day out, allowed me to mature some in the way I did handle the public once I got into the Highway Patrol.

This time period also allowed me to attend San Antonio Junior College at nights to further my education. The federal government had a grant program that paid the tuition and books for courses as long as you stayed in law enforcement for a period of at least two years after completing the government-funded course. After I transferred to the Highway Patrol, I continued going to college, and attended Odessa College at night. I stayed with getting my college education until I had to start taking English and government classes to proceed, at which point I figured I had gone to college long enough.

Training to be a Texas Highway Patrolman, we all had our own notion of what the law enforcement profession would entail. After finishing the basic school, I guess all I could think of was exciting times, driving high speed cars and catching traffic violators. I don't remember any type training or classes that could have prepared us mentally for things that were to come. We were told as patrolmen we were expected to take care of everything that happened "between the fences." I guess that meant our emotions too. As we each got into our own career, we all seemed to handle emotional things a little differently, each in our own private way.

I did get to do about all I could have dreamed for in law enforcement—high speed chases, work the crime scenes, arrest criminals and law violators, security assignments—all of it. But I also had to accept that at the end of the day, it wasn't necessarily over. I just took it home with me.

Some of the things I saw and experienced, I could not talk to Linda or other family members about. Information had to be kept quiet either because of the sensitivity of the investigation or because it was considered confidential. Often there were violent episodes we witnessed in our investigations, some of them so violent and graphic that even if I could, I didn't want to share them with my family. I wanted to keep them from worrying about me and my job. And of course, I would never talk with another officer about anything bothering me emotionally. I felt that would show some type of weakness on my part. My choice was to "just suck it up and do it."

I developed a persona that gave the appearance that nothing really bothered me. I could be at a horrific crime scene with mutilated bodies and make jokes or talk about an upcoming vacation, pretending the horror before me was nothing. I would say the vast majority of the officers—if they had been in law enforcement for any length of time—put up this same front. In my time, we were never encouraged to share our feelings or emotions with mental health professionals.

The reason I want to touch on this particular subject matter is to give the reader a perspective of myself. I don't want the reader to get the impression I'm insensitive to the feelings of victims and families because the truth is quite the contrary. I use practical jokes and humor to relieve the stress.

Odessa and the Highway Patrol

Wow. So often throughout the years I have said, "I can't believe they pay me to do this."

What a job! I had a state agency actually send me to Odessa, give me a paycheck once a month to drive a high-speed automobile that they bought, assigned to me, paid the repair bills on, and furnished the gasoline and oil for. All I had to do was chase down traffic law violators in the rural areas around Odessa, take some type of enforcement action against them, and then repeat the process. The enforcement process usually was either a citation or custody arrest.

The years in the Highway Patrol had their moments, both on the lighter side and some more serious. Here's just a few of each.

I'd Rather Face Y'all

One night at the end of a shift, my partner Jim Edington was driving me home. It was about 2 A.M. and we were traveling east on 42nd Street in Odessa, approaching where 42nd intersects with Bonham. There was a service station on the south side of the intersection and as we got about even with it, we saw a young looking male run from the east side of the station, headed north across 42nd. He ran in front of our marked patrol car and entered the alley between Bonham and Redbud, still headed north.

Being somewhat curious of why the man was running, we turned into the alley and began to close the distance on him in a hurry. Just about the time we caught up to him, the man jumped over a six-foot cedar picket fence, into a yard on the west side of the alley. By the time we slid to a stop and were beginning to exit the car to give chase on foot, the man jumped back over the fence to where we had stopped. A large German Sheppard dog had just missed getting the man and he decided he had rather face us than the dog.

It turned out the man was a high school student and he and some friends had been siphoning gas out of some cars parked at the station for repairs. After a call to his parents, we sent him on his way.

Well, Maybe Not as Tough as We Were Led to Believe

In patrol school we were kind of led to believe as Highway Patrolmen we could handle anything that came down the pike in our assigned area. It made us feel proud to be wearing that uniform and going about our business of enforcing the law. We were young and "tough." It was a "macho" feeling, you might say.

One holiday, I think it was Christmas day, my partner Dennis Riley and I were working routine patrol when we got a call from the DPS dispatcher to go to the hospital in Odessa. A fellow patrolman's wife was in labor and having a difficult childbirth. They needed blood for her—right now!

Dennis and I went into the hospital to give our blood. We were big, tough Highway Patrolmen—ready to roll up our long sleeves and help our fellow patrolman's poor wife.

Two nurses ushered us into a room with two beds and told us to lie down. Dennis's nurse started to work on him first, got him stuck, and began the process of drawing blood. My nurse started drawing my blood several minutes after the process on Dennis had begun. There was all the usual bravado talk you would expect. "No pain," we bragged. "Take all you need," we offered. "Start pumping, we can handle it," we said.

The nurses both stepped out of our room for a few minutes, then, in a little bit, my nurse came back in and started unplugging me. A minute or so later Dennis's nurse came back into the room and as soon as she came through the door, she looked down at Dennis and exclaimed in a fairly loud tone, "Oh my God!"

Well that was the wrong choice of words. Dennis turned white as a sheet and he broke out into a cold sweat!

Dennis told me later from what the nurse said and the way she said it, it really scared him. He immediately thought she had drained all his blood out onto the floor. After all, he said, they had started him before me and I was already finished.

In reality what had happened is the nurse had forgotten to turn Dennis's drain on and he had not bled one drop. Even after he was revived with cold wet towels and orange juice, he did not give any blood that day.

Get It Yourself

Here's another blood drawing incident that happened to me as a young Highway Patrolman.

You didn't have to work very long on patrol before you were called to investigate a fatal accident. There is certain basic protocol to follow in accident investigation and we were thoroughly trained to handle these investigations. One of the things called for in these accidents is a blood test on all drivers and victims. We were blessed with some great Justices of the Peace who went out their way to help us get these blood tests.

My first fatal accident involved a male victim who was also the driver of the vehicle.

The victim had been removed from the scene before I arrived. He was taken to Medical Center Hospital by ambulance, where he was pronounced dead on arrival.

I finished my preliminary investigation at the scene then went to the hospital to get the victim's information and the blood specimen that had been ordered by the Justice of the Peace.

After I had gotten the driver information I needed for my report, I stood outside the emergency room where the victim was to wait for a nurse to come by so I could ask her to draw the blood specimen. I was young, dressed in my official Highway Patrol uniform, feeling pretty important.

In a little bit, an older nurse walked by. I hailed her down, told her who I was, and asked her if she would draw the blood specimen from the victim for me. She hardly slowed from her walk, just kind of looked at me, and kept going with no verbal response at all. In a minute or so the same nurse walked back by me, this time going in the opposite direction. As she walked by she didn't really look my way, but she did hand me a syringe, and at the same time she said, "Try the big toe," and she just kept on walking.

I did try the big toe, but never got any blood. I did finally get a specimen, but now I don't remember how.

Never Get Complacent

I was working days by myself and that afternoon I got a call from the Ector County Sheriff's Office advising someone, possibly a pedestrian victim of a hit-and-run accident, was lying in the grass just off of Interstate 20 and Grant. I traveled to the location and did find a man lying face down in the grass. Several truck drivers were standing nearby. They had been the ones who called the sheriff's office. The man was not conscious, but I could see no visible injuries. After I shook him a little, he woke up and he appeared to just be intoxicated. I got him up and asked him for identification, but he didn't have any. He said his name was John Jones. I arrested the man for public intoxication, patted him down and placed him in my patrol car. I transported him to the county jail, inventoried his property and filled out the booking papers. In those days it was very common for us to book our own prisoners, get the keys to the cells, and lock the prisoner up, so that's what I did.

Later that night, we had some friends over and were playing cards when I got another call from the sheriff's office. The deputy asked me if I had searched the guy "real good" before locking him in the cell. I told him I felt like I had. Then the deputy said they had received a call from a woman and she had said the man had given me a false name and that he was wanted in North Carolina for robbery and attempted murder. She had also said the man usually carried a two-shot derringer in his pocket. The deputy told me they had gone to the woman's house and found the holster for the derringer, but not the derringer. He requested I go back to the location where I had arrested the guy and see if I could locate the derringer. If I couldn't find the derringer, the deputy said, they would have to perform a search of the entire Ector County Jail.

I did go back to the location on Interstate 20 and within a matter of minutes located the derringer, fully loaded, lying on the ground at the exact spot where the suspect had been. It appeared "John Jones" must have been lying on the gun when the truck drivers and I approached him and left it there when he got up. Had I been by myself, who knows what the man would have attempted to do?

Welcomed Change in Patrol Assignment

One security and enforcement assignment I really enjoyed occurred in the fall of 1976. This assignment also gave me the opportunity to work with my brother Skipper for the first time.

Skipper decided to start a career with the DPS after he finished college. He started the DPS Law Enforcement Academy in the fall of 1975 and graduated in March of 1976. He was assigned to Highway Patrol Service in McCamey, Texas, and his partner was Sammy Long.

An annual chili cook-off at Terlingua, Texas, a small town south of Alpine on the Rio Grande, had been held for several years back then. Every year the cook-off seemed to grow and become a little more rowdy. In addition to the normal competing chili cooks, there were a lot of young people who used the cook-off as an excuse to come down and camp out, party, drink lots of alcohol and do some things outside the law. We had heard that at the fall of 1975 cook-off, a woman had been brutally raped by intoxicated men camped at the event.

So, for the fall of 1976 cook-off, it was decided to also have a very large law enforcement presence. A small army of law enforcement personnel descended on the town of Terlingua. Many law enforcement agencies were represented, the Texas Department of Public Safety, the Texas Parks and Wildlife Department, the Texas Liquor Control Board, the U.S. Border Patrol and various local county agencies among them.

All law enforcement personnel met in Alpine around noon on the Friday of the cook-off weekend to be given our assignments. So there would be round-the-clock coverage, assignments were broken into two 12-hour shifts, a 6 A.M. to

Texas Ranger Joe Hunt and DPS Sergeant John (Skipper) Hunt

6 P.M. day shift and a 6 P.M. to 6 A.M. night watch. Highway Patrolmen, for the most part, were assigned a specific stretch of roadway leading from Alpine to Terlingua. That's the assignment Skipper and Sammy were given, and they got the night shift. Since they were pretty much locked into just patrolling their assigned area and could not leave the area for two long nights, it was a pretty boring assignment.

I lucked out in my assignment. I was toward the end of the drawing and my partner, Craig Mangum, and I got a rover assignment on the night shift. This turned out to be the best assignment you could get. We patrolled everywhere, from the cook-off site to Terlingua, looking for any and all type of violations. We actually arrested one of the first violators Friday evening, a very intoxicated young male. The U.S. Border Patrol had brought a bus down to transport prisoners back to Alpine and a temporary cage had been brought in to lock up violators until there were enough to make the bus trip worthwhile. A Justice of the Peace was on duty at the law enforcement command center close to the cook-off. Class C misdemeanor violations that did not include intoxication or speed were mostly taken to the judge by custody arrest and disposed of then and there. Lots of people saw the judge that weekend. Both Craig and I really enjoyed the break from our routine patrol duties and the opportunity to work with other agencies and officers in restoring some type of order to this event.

The law enforcement presence made its statement that year. The following year, there was not near the number of law enforcement officers and patrolmen as the year before, but

the worst and the rowdiest party-goers stayed away also.
The cook-off returned to a more family-oriented event that
could be enjoyed without the lawless crowd that had been
showing up.

Sammy's Last Stop

On Wednesday, November 17, 1976, I was working days on Highway Patrol in Odessa. Skipper and Sammy were in Odessa getting their patrol car repaired at French Tool Plymouth dealership in Odessa. I met them and during the meeting, Skipper told me he was going to ask his sergeant, Leon Roberts, for a holiday leave day on Sunday, November 21, 1976. If he got the day off approved, he was going to go with his wife Cindi to San Angelo because our family was having a baby shower for them. Skipper did tell me he wasn't sure he could get the day off approved because Sgt. Roberts didn't necessarily like them taking regular assigned weekends off. After Skip and Sammy left Odessa that day I did not talk to him again, so I did not know if he had gotten the day off approved or not.

Late in the afternoon that Sunday, I had just gotten off duty and was watching television in the living room at home in Odessa. The telephone rang and I answered it in the kitchen. Jim Swain, a Highway Patrolman stationed in Midland, said

"Joe, we are hearing radio traffic from the sheriff's office in Upton County and they are dispatching deputies to a location out of Rankin. They are reporting that both Highway Patrolmen have been shot." Jim told me they were hearing the traffic on the sheriff's office frequency, not the DPS frequency and that was all he knew at that time.

Immediately I tried to call my parents' home in San Angelo to see if Skipper was in fact there. The line was busy, so I hung up and called my parents' neighbor, Willie Englert, and asked him to go tell my parents to call me as soon as possible. In just a minute or two my mother called and she confirmed Skipper was in San Angelo and he and Cindi were there at the house. I told Skip what Jim had relayed to me and said I would call Jim back, try to get an update, and call him right back.

When I called Jim back he told me deputies had reached the scene and were reporting Sammy Long and a second person had been shot. According to the radio traffic, Jim said it appeared Sammy was dead at the scene. He wasn't sure on the second person's condition or identity.

I called Skip back as I had promised. He said he would leave immediately for Rankin and I told him I would meet him there. I called my sergeant, O.A. Brookshire, told him what was going on and told him I was going to Rankin to be with Skipper. I then called Dennis Riley, my Highway Patrol partner. Dennis said he wanted to ride with me to Rankin. I called Jim again and he confirmed Sammy was dead from gunshot wounds. The second person who was shot appeared to be the person who shot Sammy. Jim told me other DPS personnel from Midland were en route to Rankin, but apparently the only suspect involved was in custody. After getting my uniform on, I picked Dennis up at his house and we headed to Rankin, about 65 miles southeast of Odessa.

I don't remember much more about that night. I don't know if we got to Rankin before Skip or not. We went to the sheriff's office or courthouse—I don't remember which, just that it was where all the other officers were gathered. I do remember seeing Texas Ranger Charlie Hodges there and we spoke just briefly. I had just made the list for Texas Ranger.

After getting to Rankin, I did get a few more facts on how the events had unfolded that Sunday evening and what made Jim think both patrolmen had been shot when they heard the first radio traffic.

Sammy got a speeding pickup on radar that was headed east on U.S. Highway 67 out of Rankin. He evidently had to chase the pickup for some distance from Rankin, finally getting it stopped several miles east of there. According to witness reports, as Sammy approached the pickup, the driver exited the pickup and shot Sammy at point blank range. Sammy ran to the back of his patrol car and collapsed. A deer hunter returning to San Angelo from a hunting trip with his son witnessed what was happening from a roadside park about 100 yards west of where the traffic stop was made.

The suspect, a black male, followed Sammy to the rear of his patrol car, retrieved Sammy's service revolver from his holster, then stood over Sammy and shot him six more times, killing him. As the suspect stood there shooting Sammy, the deer hunter got out his rifle and began to shoot at the suspect, hitting him several times. The suspect retreated from the back of Sammy's patrol car to the front of his pickup and collapsed there. He was taken to the hospital in Rankin where he died about 45 minutes after arriving there. Sammy was pronounced dead at the scene by an Upton County Justice of the Peace.

Another witness, a female college student, drove upon the scene and called the Upton County Sheriff's Office on her CB radio. She at first reported a Highway Patrolman had just been shot, then immediately corrected her statement and said, "No, there have been two shot," meaning the patrolman and the suspect. The dispatcher in Rankin knew Sammy and Skipper were partners so she assumed when the student said two had been shot, it was both partners. The dispatcher reported to deputies that both patrolmen had been shot and that was the initial dispatch the Midland DPS Communications Center heard.

After meeting with Skipper and getting the information, we went to the funeral home to view Sammy. He was lying face down with his uniform pants on, his Sam Browne belt and holster on, and a white tee shirt. The shots the suspect fired from Sammy's service revolver had evidently struck Sammy in the lower back. Some had penetrated the Sam Browne belt.

At the conclusion of the investigation, the case was presented to the Upton County grand jury. The deer hunter was no-billed by the grand jury; the shooting of the suspect was determined to be justifiable. The deer hunter's identity was to remain secret, and has been kept sealed.

Skipper was present during some of the proceedings and he was aware of the identity of the deer hunter, but he never told me the hunter's name nor did I ever ask.

Meeting the Deer Hunter

Years later, I was Tom Green County Sheriff, and I finally got to meet the "Deer Hunter." It was late in the afternoon, February 27, 2007, and Lt. Bill Fiveash came into my office. Bill asked me if I would like to meet the "Deer Hunter." Bill knew the man, but of course I had never met him. Only in the last year or so had I heard his name because an open records request had been filed to try and get the man's name released. The man came into the sheriff's office, Bill introduced him to me, and we visited for about 30 minutes. Skipper was in a school in Austin, so he was not in town, but we made arrangements to take the "Hunter" out to dinner the next week, after Skipper returned home.

On March 2, 2007, a Friday evening, Linda and I, Skipper and his wife Linda and the "Hunter" all went to eat supper together. It was the first time Skipper had seen him since they had met during the 1976 Grand Jury proceedings. The "Hunter" lived out of state and had for quite some time, but he was in San Angelo visiting family and friends.

The "Hunter" talked some about the incident the evening of Nov. 21, 1976. He said he had first seen the male suspect at a convenience store located at the Interstate 10 and Interstate 20 split near Kent, Texas. He noticed the man just kind of hanging around, but said he didn't think a lot of it at that time. After the shooting was over, he said he was made aware the pickup the suspect was driving was stolen and that the man had a "criminal past." Learning the suspect had a criminal past made the "Hunter" wonder if the man had been waiting around the store to rob it, but had given up because too many people kept coming in.

The "Hunter" told us he and his son continued on toward San Angelo and just east of Rankin, the same man they had seen at the store passed them in the pickup, followed by the Highway Patrolman. Evidently, he said, the patrolman was chasing the pickup. As the pickup and the patrol car pulled off to the side of the road, he pulled into the roadside park on the opposite side of the road. Almost immediately, the "Hunter" realized the Patrolman was running toward the rear of his car and the pickup driver was chasing him. He saw Sammy fall down. Then he saw the man shooting him.

At first the "Hunter" said he thought the pistol shots were missing Sammy because each time the suspect took a shot, he could see dirt flying up off the ground. He thought if he could shoot the man, he would save the Patrolman's life since the first round of bullets had probably missed. He wasn't aware that the rounds were actually hitting Sammy until the incident was over and the preliminary investigation was done.

Skipper and I just let the "Hunter" talk without asking many questions. He explained that he was not sure he was hitting the man because he did not fall down. He told his son to keep the jeep in gear and be ready to go in case the man got back into his pickup and came after them.

He showed us a card he had received from Col. Wilson Speir after the incident. It looked like an unlined index card and it had "Mr. Deer Hunter, a special friend of the Texas Department of Public Safety" written on it. It was signed by Col. Speir. The card was tattered and worn and Skipper offered to get him a new card signed by the current DPS Director, Col. Tommy Davis.

Skipper did arrange for Col. Davis to issue a new card in April of 2007. It also certified Mr. Deer Hunter was a special friend of the DPS for his attempt to save Sammy Long's life in the incident on November 21, 1976. The card was mailed to "The Hunter."

Before the "Hunter" left that April, I invited him to our ranch in Schleicher County to hunt white-tail deer any time he could get back our way.

On January 6, 2008, he returned to San Angelo for a visit and came out and hunted for several days at our ranch. It was a special season for does and spikes and the "Hunter" was successful in killing two does. This was the first time he had hunted deer in about six years, he told me, and he seemed to thoroughly enjoy every day he got to hunt. I enjoyed visiting with him.

After that, he came back to our ranch every year to hunt. Two years in a row he shot a deer stand my son had made and I kidded him that I thought he had shot more deer stands than deer.

Sadly, the "Hunter" passed away March 11, 2013. He suffered a massive stroke and thankfully he didn't linger but a couple of days before the Lord took him home.

"The Hunter" and Taylor Hunt
Hunt Ranch, January 2008

Drunk to Drunk

It doesn't take long working an area like Odessa to make several arrests on the same individual. I arrested several of the same people several times over the years. Here is just one of those occasions.

I'm not trying to blow my own horn, but I always worked under the theory of treating people the way I would like to be treated, and I tried to treat my contacts in a civil manner. I very seldom had any altercations when making arrests and I credit that to this theory. Many violators have actually thanked me after I have issued them a citation or made a custody arrest. Treating people this way was drilled into us by the DPS and I believe, at that time, most Highway Patrolmen adhered to that standard procedure.

One night I got behind a "drunk car" going south toward Odessa on U.S. Highway 385. The vehicle was doing the usual things, weaving from lane to lane, driving slow, etc. I turned on my red lights and got the vehicle stopped five to six miles north of Odessa. As I approached the suspect vehicle, a man I recognized as Dearl Flowers exited the car. I had arrested Dearl some years back for DWI and he was apparently drunk again. He recognized me and we exchanged pleasantries.

I told Dearl that his driving had drawn me to him and by observing and talking with him; I felt he had had too much to drink to be driving. I told him I was placing him under arrest for DWI and would take him to the DPS office to administer a breath test. Dearl was as cooperative as he could be.

I got Dearl into my patrol car, secured his car and began our trip into the Odessa office.

I had not gone a mile when I came up on another "drunk car." It was the same thing, driving real slow and weaving back and forth so I turned on my red lights and got that vehicle stopped.

I got the driver out of the vehicle and it appeared he had had more alcohol to drink than Dearl. I arrested him for DWI and since I had at least dealt with Dearl in the past, I felt it would be safer to put Dearl in the backseat of the patrol car behind the front passenger seat and put the second suspect in the front seat with me. I did this and away we went to the DPS office.

All the way to the DPS office the newest suspect was really vocal, cursing me, making threats, etc. That is not unusual for intoxicated subjects.

When we got to the office, I got both Dearl and the other suspect into the building. I sat them across from each other at a long table we used to do reports on. I then got the breathalyzer out of its secured cabinet, plugged it in, and began to prepare it for testing. While I was doing all this, the new suspect was really giving me some verbal abuse.

The abuse went on for several minutes. Then, all of a sudden, Dearl kind of rose up from his seat and leaned over toward this suspect. "Look, that man down there (talking about me) is just doing his job in trying to save our lives and if you don't shut up, I'm going to come across this table and whip your a--." I never heard another peep out of the suspect.

Months after that, I had been working nights and was home asleep. The telephone rang and it was Dearl. He told me he was at the Ector County Attorney's office and they had offered him a six-month probated jail term and fine for his DWI I filed. He asked me what I thought and I told him it did not sound like a bad deal to me.

"Mr. Hunt, there isn't any way I can go for six months and not go to a bar to drink," Dearl said. I told him that probably the only other option would be to take the jail time, usually three days, and not be on probation. Dearl said that was what he would do, and he did.

Your Honor

One of the first men I met when I transferred to the Highway Patrol in Odessa in 1970 was Jan Brooks. Our meeting turned into a life-long friendship that lasted until Jan died the day after Christmas in 2012.

When I first met Jan, he had just bought Permian Wrecker Service and rotated with other wrecking service companies in Odessa working traffic accidents for the Highway Patrol. But also he would pick up our custody arrest vehicles once we had removed the driver from that vehicle.

Some years later, Jan decided he would like to try his hand at politics. Jan ran for Justice of the Peace in his precinct. He won the election and took office two to three years before I left for the Texas Rangers.

Now, back then, if someone from another state got a misdemeanor traffic citation while they were visiting Texas, and if they went back home without paying the fine or appearing in court, they were likely to get away with it. Since Texas did not have interstate agreements with other states, those who received citations were not required by their home state to take care of the citations once they returned home.

Of course that meant if a Texas Highway Patrolman wrote a ticket on a person from out of state, we usually would never get a disposition on that ticket. The only way we could to take care of the situation was to custody arrest the violator so he could appear before a Justice of the Peace. If it was after hours and the JP had gone home for the day, it was usually the following day before the court appearance could be arranged. Most JP's did not like to be called out after hours or on weekends.

But Jan did not mind being called out after hours and on weekends. After he was elected, we were able to make more custody arrests, especially on out-of-state speeders and get them before a judge, no matter what time of day or night it was.

Jan also liked riding with all the Highway Patrolmen when he could. One night he was riding with me, the sun had not been down long and I got a truck on my radar on Interstate 20 that was speeding. I stopped the truck and the driver was from out of state.

I advised the truck driver that since he was from out of state, he was being arrested for speeding and it would be required he be taken before a Justice of the Peace immediately to enter a plea on the charge. I instructed him to park his tractor-trailer on a motel parking lot along the interstate so he would not have to take the rig downtown. The driver got in the front seat of my patrol car with me and Jan moved to the rear passenger seat behind him. We started our trip downtown to the courthouse and there was not a lot of conversation. The truck driver did express his concerns about "out of state" justice he was probably about to experience. He had heard of the railroad-type justice from other drivers across the country. Jan never said a word all the way to the courthouse.

When we got to the courthouse, the truck driver followed me to the general office area of the four Justices of the Peace. Jan walked around both of us and went in his office and sat down behind his desk.

The truck driver looked at me with this kind of lost look and then went into Jan's office as I had motioned. Jan started all the preliminaries of introducing himself to the driver as Justice Peace Brooks, courts in session, etc. and you could just see the air leaving the truck driver.

Jan informed the man of the charge against him and of his options to plead guilty or post a bond. I thought Jan was very professional and courteous to the man. The man pleaded guilty, paid a fine and we took him back to his truck. I think by the way the man was treated that night that he had to leave with a different—and possibly improved—opinion of our judicial system.

Opportunities in the Highway Patrol and Rangers

Being a commissioned officer in the DPS and Texas Rangers afforded some opportunities officers with other departments didn't necessarily have. I guess what really opened the door for these opportunities were the fact that DPS Patrolmen and Rangers have statewide jurisdiction in enforcing Texas State Laws. Consequently, assignments could be made to other parts of the state for temporary duty in some very high profile incidents. These assignments could be for natural disasters, criminal activities, or security assignments.

I did not have many instances in the Highway Patrol to go to a natural disaster. Actually, I only traveled one time for a natural disaster. In about 1976, I was sent to Monahans and spent one night patrolling the area. A small tornado had touched down and done some damage. The next day I returned to my home station in Odessa.

By the Hair of My Chinny, Chin, Chin

I did miss a natural disaster assignment in the fall of 1970. A pretty good hurricane was headed for Texas and my sergeant, O.A. (Bob) Brookshire, called me and said that my partner, Ed White, and I were on standby to go down to the coast when the hurricane actually came ashore. It was coming up for our long weekend off, Friday through Monday, and I had already planned to take my family to San Angelo that weekend. I asked Sgt. Brookshire if I could go on to San Angelo and have Ed just pick me up there if we got the call while I was there, but he would not approve that.

Later that day, I was talking to Ed at the DPS office in Odessa. Jack Wasson, another Highway Patrolman, was there and "ragging" me because I was going to have to go to the coast. Jack also knew I had planned to go to San Angelo for the weekend and he kind of rubbed it in that I wasn't going to get to go. Jack and I were in the same Highway Patrol school in the first part of 1967 so I guess you could say there was a little rivalry there. Jack told me he had already been sent to the coast for security duty after a hurricane in the fall of 1967 and it was my turn to go.

The next day, Sgt. Brookshire called and said it did not look like the hurricane was going to be as severe as they had predicted. All the patrolmen from Region 4-A had been taken off of standby status. I asked Sgt. Brookshire if that meant I could now take my family to San Angelo for my long weekend. He said that would be fine.

I did just that. The family and I went to San Angelo and had a good time. Monday afternoon, we were returning to Odessa between Sterling City and Garden City, and about 10 miles west of Sterling City, I met Jack Wasson and Ed White. Jack was driving his Highway Patrol unit and he had it "eared back" with both antennas on the back of the car lying almost on top of the trunk. Jack had an old "scowly" look on his face and both hands gripping the top of the steering wheel. He never saw me. He was going too fast.

I got back to Odessa and learned that after I left for San Angelo, the DPS decided more Highway Patrolmen were going to be needed for the hurricane duty. So the call went out. Jack happened to be in Odessa and he got the call to go with Ed. Believe me, I got to hear some harsh words from Jack when he returned from that assignment.

Promotion to the Rangers

In Texas, I believe there are a lot of law enforcement officers who would like to promote to Texas Rangers. Not too many years before I promoted, officers from outside agencies were promoted to the Rangers on occasion. This was primarily while Col. Homer Garrison was the DPS director, but there were some Col. Wilson Speir promoted after Col. Garrison's death. Once in the DPS, I certainly had my ambitions to be a Texas Ranger.

In 1974 I began to study so that in the future I could compete for a promotion to the Rangers. The promotion process at that time consisted of a written test and oral interview board. The written test was given at regional DPS offices around the state. The interview board convened in Austin. You had to be in the top scores statewide on your written test to get called to go before the oral board.

At the time I tested, you had to have at least eight years law enforcement experience, and the last several years of that had to be in the DPS. When I applied and tested for the first time in 1975, I had just over eight years experience. I scored high enough on the written test to go to the oral board, but my overall score that year was too low to be placed on the eligibility list for promotion.

I was fortunate in 1976, the second year I tested. Again, I scored high enough on the written test to be called to Austin before the interview board. Six people made up the interview board and three of the six were Texas Rangers. Generally the Senior Ranger Captain or his assistant chaired the board and that year it was the senior captain.

The board evaluated the answers to their questions and also reviewed the applicant's work history and supervisor's evaluations and they established an eligibility list of five candidates for promotions. That list was good for one year. It didn't expire until November of 1977. With the combination of my written test score, oral interview score and service points, I came out fifth overall in the state. I was Number 5 on the list.

On January 1, 1977, Numbers 1, 2 and 3 were promoted to Texas Rangers. This left me Number 2 on a list with nearly a full year ahead of me. Joe Wylie was the one ahead of me. He was promoted to Ranger in about April of 1977 and that moved me to the only one on the list. Joe Wylie's Ranger duty station was Amarillo. Then, in July of 1977, I was promoted to Ranger.

I remember the telephone call I received from Senior Capt. Bill Wilson, telling me my promotion date would be July. He also said the actual opening was in Houston, but that a Ranger in Lubbock needed to move to the valley to care for his sick in-laws. Capt. Wilson told me he would give me the choice between Houston and Lubbock for my Ranger station. I responded, "Captain, you are just giving me a sanity test to see if I am still eligible for the Rangers. Of course I'll take Lubbock." Capt. Wilson laughed and said that would be a good choice.

TEXAS DEPARTMENT OF PUBLIC SAFETY
5805 N. LAMAR BLVD. - BOX 4087 - AUSTIN, TEXAS 78773

WILSON E. SPEIR
DIRECTOR

LEO E. GOSSETT
ASST. DIRECTOR

COMMISSION
OTTIS E. LOCK
CHAIRMAN
ROBERT R. SHELTON
WILLIAM B. BLAKEMORE, II
COMMISSIONERS

June 22, 1977

Joe Burl Hunt
Trooper II
Highway Patrol Service
Texas Department of Public Safety
Box 647
Odessa, Texas 79760

Dear Trooper Hunt:

Congratulations on your appointment to the position of Texas Ranger, Texas Ranger Service.

Effective July 15, 1977, you will assume this position in the Criminal Law Enforcement Division under the command of Chief J. M. Ray, and Senior Captain W. D. Wilson, Texas Ranger Service. Your assignment will be Company "C" under the command of Captain W. A. Werner and your station is Lubbock.

You will be notified at a later date when to report to the Personnel and Training Bureau in Austin for the commissioning ceremony. Members of your family are welcome to attend this ceremony.

With kindest regards, I am

Sincerely yours,

Wilson E. Speir
Wilson E. Speir
Director

WES/Gs

cc: Leo E. Gossett, Assistant Director   Captain W. A. Werner
     Chief Joe E. Milner   Sergeant Orvil A. Brookshire
     Chief J. M. Ray   Sergeant William T. Newberry
     Major E. K. Browning, Jr.   Sam E. Green
     Senior Captain W. D. Wilson   Personnel and Training
     Captain Hugh Shaw

COURTESY • SERVICE • PROTECTION

Letter of Promotion to Texas Ranger

Sr. Capt. Bill Wilson, Chief Ray, Col. Gossett, Joe Hunt, Col. Speir

Ranger Security Assignments, Special Investigations

Most of the security assignments I was involved with in the Rangers involved the governor or his family. This occurred when the governor or his wife were traveling to our assigned area for an event. We were usually available to drive either one as we were familiar with the roads in our area. By doing this, we were also available to assist members of the Governor Security Detail if they needed help while in our area.

Texas Gov. George Bush and his wife Laura were far and away ahead of any governor and wife I was ever around. Both were down to earth, laid back people who genuinely respected others.

My least favorite governor and wife, well … I'm not going to go there.

Special investigations, those conducted on elected officials and other police officers accused of law violations, were assigned to us out of Austin. Some accusations were founded. Some were not. What made these investigations sad were the usual net gains the suspects obtained. Most often, the financial gains were minimal considering what it cost the individual in disgrace.

Governor George Bush, Texas Ranger Joe Hunt
Governor Security, San Angelo, TX., October 1998

Governor for a Day

One assignment my wife Linda and I were able to be a part of and enjoy occurred in Austin, Texas. I think every year that the legislature is in session, the governor gets to choose a person to be "Governor for a Day." We had a very popular senator from Lubbock by the name of John T. Montford and in April of 1993, Gov. Ann Richards selected Sen. Montford to be the "Governor for a Day." For that weekend, Gov. Richards was supposedly out-of-state and Sen. Montford was at the capitol on her behalf.

At that time Jackie Peoples and I were both Rangers in Lubbock. We had worked with Sen. Montford when he was the district attorney in Lubbock, and for some unknown reason, we had earned his respect. Sen. Montford requested Jackie and I accompany him as his security for the weekend in Austin. He also invited us to bring our wives, Linda and Shelby. The events of the weekend started about mid-day on Friday and ended after lunch on Sunday. As the details of what the weekend involved, it became evident there would be some fairly good expenses for Jackie and me to stay in the same hotel and eat at the same restaurants as other state officials attending the event.

Also, there was a Saturday night event that required a tuxedo. Our captain, Charlie Moore called the senior captain in Austin and told him of Sen. Montford's invitation and the expenses that would be involved. The senior captain approved all of our expenses, including the rental of the tuxedo. Jackie and I were to turn in all actual costs, with receipts, so that we could be reimbursed.

A side note to this story was that this was while the Branch Davidian investigation was at its height. Just a day or two before Jackie and I got our tuxedos, Ranger Bill Gerth had called Capt. Moore on behalf of the Rangers in Company "C" who were processing the crime scene in Waco after the fire. Ranger Gerth told Capt. Moore the Rangers were ruining their clothes sifting through all of the debris that remained from the Branch Davidian fire. Capt. Moore got the request approved for coveralls for the Rangers processing the crime scene.

Just the next day or the day after, Jackie and I were fitted for our tuxedos and we picked them up. We had some pictures taken of us in our tuxedos and I remember sending a copy of my tuxedo picture to Ranger Gerth, who was a friend. I told Bill he was not the only one who had to order special uniforms for "line of duty" work and "reminded" him that the nature of the assignment, whether it's digging through ashes or attending fancy banquets at the capitol, dictates what kind of special uniform Austin needs to buy for its officers.

This is just another one of those opportunities I would have never had if I had not been in the DPS.

John T. Montford
Governor for a Day
April 24, 1993

Rear: Ranger Joe Hunt, Senator John T. Montford, Ranger Jackie Peoples
Front: Linda Hunt, Shelby Peoples

Friendships as Results of Investigations (Beatrice Jacobo)

Where do I start? There are so many. I guess when tragedy hits a family and a law enforcement reaction is needed to help make a final resolution, it just makes for a special kind of bond between the victims and the officers involved.

The first incident I want to share is a fatal traffic accident involving a hit-and-run driver I worked while on the Highway Patrol in Ector County.

On the evening of April 19, 1973, I was called to a major accident in what was called the South Ranchito Addition, a small housing addition just south of Odessa, but in Ector County. By the time we got to the scene, a young girl, 12-year-old Beatrice Jacobo was already dead. Beatrice had been walking beside her bicycle with her brother and had been struck by a car with such a violent impact her right leg had been completely severed from her hip.

The driver of the car failed to stop at the scene of the accident, but I got enough of a description on the suspect vehicle to make an area-wide broadcast for an attempt to locate. Not long after the broadcast, an Odessa Police officer found a vehicle at a car wash similar to the one described in the broadcast. The vehicle had blood on the outside of it and the young man washing the car told the officer he had just hit a dog.

Lab analysis positively identified the vehicle as the one that hit Beatrice and the man washing the vehicle was identified as the driver of the vehicle. He subsequently pleaded guilty to failure to stop and render aid and negligent homicide and was sentenced to five years in prison.

Beatrice's father, Sostenes Jacobo, was especially grateful for how quickly the suspect was apprehended and for all the investigation techniques used to identify the suspect driver and vehicle. I spent many hours collecting evidence from the vehicle, hand delivering the evidence to the DPS lab in Austin for analysis and putting the case together for presentation to the Grand Jury for indictment. During all of this process, I stayed in contact with the Jacobo family, updating them on events as they came about.

After the prosecution of the defendant was complete, I did not have much more contact with the Jacobo family. I just knew that during the time period from the accident to the prosecution, they were very appreciative of the efforts of the investigation and updates.

One night months after the Jacobo accident, I was working routine patrol South of Odessa on U.S. Highway 385 and came across a motorist having radiator trouble. I got the motorist in my vehicle and went to Neal Pool Wrecking located on the northeast corner of South Grant and Clements in the south part of Odessa. We filled a jug with some water for the radiator and got ready to head back to where the disabled vehicle was. As I left the wrecking yard, there wasn't any traffic traveling north and south, but there was a vehicle headed east and stopped in the inside lane of Clements. I assumed it was stopped for the red light at that intersection. I pulled diagonally across the intersection, headed south, and a pickup truck came from behind the stopped vehicle. It was headed east on Clements. As it turned out, the traffic light was green for traffic eastbound on Clements. I guess the stopped vehicle had seen my patrol car easing out into the intersection and had just stopped to give me the right of way.

The collision wasn't too shabby. It really did a number on the right rear quarter panel of my patrol car. The pickup truck was an older model and had a really heavy-duty bumper and grill guard on the front of it. This bumper guard is what really did the damage to my vehicle. I got out of my vehicle, and as I rounded the front of my car I saw the passenger in the pickup getting out of his seat. He was holding his neck and groaning. But then, I then made eye contact with the driver of the pickup, who was also getting out of his seat. What a coincidence. It was Mr. Jacobo. I asked Mr. Jacobo if he was all right and he said he was, and he said his passenger was all right too.

The damage to Mr. Jacobo's pickup was primarily the front bumper and grill guard. He didn't want to, but he finally agreed to let the DPS pay for him a new bumper. I'm convinced that once he saw I was the driver of the patrol car he did not want to pursue any type of litigation. I was totally in the wrong and had it been a different driver in the pickup that night, I'm pretty sure things would have been a little different.

Sometimes When You Are Young Things Just Don't Add Up

In about February of 1982, I received a call from Garza County Reserve Deputy Bobby Dean. He had arrested two people on a minor in possession of alcohol (beer) charges. Also, Dean explained, the two were in possession of a pickup truck and he wanted help interviewing them about its ownership.

I got to Post and found out Dean had been patrolling county roads in west Garza County when he came upon a pickup displaying Nevada license plates. The driver of the pickup was Darren Keith Yaws, 20. Yaws' passenger was Mary Frances Miller, 19. Dean was suspicious about the out-of-state plates. He watched Yaws drive the pickup to the end of a dead end road and as he was in the process of turning it around, Dean made the initial stop. Once Dean determined Yaws and Miller were underage and drinking beer, Dean made the arrest and Yaws and Miller were in custody in the Garza County Jail.

The pickup was registered to a Joseph Wedemeyer in Nevada and neither Yaws nor Miller could quite agree on how they came to be in possession of it.

Quite a few personal-type papers addressed to Wedemeyer were found in the pickup. I interviewed Yaws and then Miller, talking to each one for a while and I wasn't convinced of their explanation of buying the pickup from Wedemeyer at a gambling casino in Nevada.

Next I talked with other Nevada law enforcement officials, then Wedemeyer's relatives and friends. Their feelings were Wedemeyer had probably met with foul play. I interviewed Miller again the next day and got a statement from her.

Wedemeyer had picked Yaws and Miller up hitch hiking in Nevada. While they were riding along, Wedemeyer showed them a pistol he had hidden under the front seat. North of Mojave, Calif., Wedemeyer got sleepy and let Yaws drive and as Wedemeyer slept, Yaws retrieved the pistol and shot Wedemeyer.

While still a few miles north of Mojave, Miller said they disposed of Wedemeyer's body near a county road, which she described in detail.

I called the sheriff's office in Mojave, and asked the deputy who answered if a body had been found north of town. He advised no body had been found.

I explained I had a statement from a suspect, and gave the deputy directions to the county road where Miller said they had disposed of Wedemeyer's body. "I know that exact location," the deputy said.

Within 30 minutes, I got a return phone call from the deputy. They had found Wedemeyer's body in the location and position Miller had described.

Shortly thereafter I got a phone call from Dwight Pendleton, a Kern County California Sheriff's Office investigator, advising that murder warrants were being issued for Yaws and Miller.

I agreed to serve the warrants as soon as we received them, and, at Pendleton's request, I also agreed to transport Yaws and Miller to the Lubbock County Jail so they could be interviewed by the California investigators when they arrived in Lubbock.

I transported Miller to the Lubbock County Jail that afternoon by car.

The following day, DPS Helicopter Pilot Dave Wansley flew me and Texas Ranger Warren Yeager to Garza County to pick up Yaws and transport him back to the Lubbock County Jail.

We had Yaws out of his cell, handcuffed with leg irons on, standing in the hall. We were talking with Garza County Sheriff Jim Pippin. Just as we were about to leave the building to go to the helicopter, Sheriff Pippin asked me if I had just a minute.

He walked into his office and retrieved an RG 38 caliber pistol he had in his top desk drawer. He asked me if I knew where he might buy some oversize grips for the pistol. I told him I didn't know, and Pippin replied, "Well, this gun sure has a good feel to it." Then, just to show me, he pointed the pistol at his desk and pulled the trigger.

BOOM. The gun discharged. The bullet bounced off Pippin's desk into some magazines stacked on his desk. Wansley and Yeager came running into the office with their guns drawn. They were not sure what was happening. We all laughed about it, though needless to say, Pippin was quite embarrassed by the ordeal.

We left the jail with Yaws and transported him back to Lubbock.

Miller and Yaws were tried separately. Miller was convicted by a jury trial and was sentenced to 15 years in prison for her part in the killing.

Months later, I was called to testify in Yaws' murder trial in Kern County, California. I testified for the prosecution and had been passed to the defense for cross examination.

One of the first things the defense brought up was the gun discharge in the Garza County Sheriff's Office and the helicopter ride back to Lubbock, accusing me of using underhanded tactics to get a confession from Yaws.

The jury didn't buy into this defense and convicted Yaws to life in prison.

Sometimes When You Are Older, It's Just Not Your Day

This entire story is strictly from memory and the reason I tell it is because of the irony of the incident. I'm sure the defendant in this murder thought he was home free after committing the murder, and he almost was.

This murder actually occurred in Lubbock sometime in the mid-1980s. Now I can't remember the name of the defendant or his wife, but the details of the case have stayed with me all these years.

The defendant killed his wife at their home, and then cut off her head, hands and feet with a chainsaw. Thinking he could hide the evidence, he dug a hole by his garage and dropped her extremities in the hole. He filled the hole partly with dirt and planted a new shrub on top of the body parts. Next he rolled the body torso up in a tarp and placed it in the trunk of his car.

He drove to a remote and seldom traveled location known as the Fluvanna Road Cut-off, located south of Post, off the highway between Post and Snyder. He parked just on top of the cap rock, which is a fairly tall hill for that country, then removed the body torso from the tarp and let it roll down the hillside.

The torso was certainly out of sight and would have probably never been found. But just as the defendant was pushing the body off the cap rock, a local rancher and one of his ranch workers were headed into Post. The rancher, Ben Miller, was too far back to tell what the defendant had thrown off the mountain, but thought it was probably a deer carcass. Miller did not stop to look at what had been thrown out, but he was curious about what was going on. By the time the defendant reached the stop sign on the Post-Snyder highway, Miller had caught up with him and was close enough behind the defendant's vehicle to record the license number, which he wrote with his finger in the dust on his dashboard. Once he had the license plate number, Miller drove back to the top of the cap rock and discovered that what the defendant had rolled down the hillside was a woman's torso. He immediately drove into Justiceburg and notified the sheriff's office in Post of his discovery.

I happened to be on my way to Post that morning and was nearly there when the call came over the radio of the body's discovery. I went directly to the scene and arrived there at the same time Garza County Deputy Billy Timms did. We determined the body was actually located in Scurry County so the Scurry County Sheriff's Office was called. Of course at that time, we had no idea where the murder had occurred or where the body was from.

The license number was checked and showed to be registered to a man in Lubbock, so Lubbock County Sheriff's Capt. Dean Bohannon drove to the address listed on the license return for the owner of the vehicle. Capt. Bohannon had just arrived at the address when the defendant drove up. He was wearing cut-off shorts and still had drops of dried blood on his legs.

Having determined the murder occurred within the Lubbock city limits, the Lubbock Police Department took over the investigation. I can't remember if the defendant was tried or pled to the murder.

Still Making Friends as the Result of an Investigation

In April of 1978, I was called to assist the Lubbock County Sheriff's Office in a murder investigation. The victim in the case was a married man, who was shot and killed while sitting with a female acquaintance in a car in a cotton field east of Lubbock. The female acquaintance managed to escape from the two perpetrators and she had run to a nearby farmhouse and reported the crime. After a fairly lengthy investigation, two defendants were arrested, charged and convicted of the murder.

During the investigation, however, I met Bobby and Carolyn Sawyer, who owned a sheet metal business in Lubbock. The male victim in this case had worked for Bobby and Carolyn, and though they didn't have any involvement or knowledge of the crime, they did provide information on the lifestyle and some habits of the employee. I guess I connected positively with Bobby and Carolyn because they were "down home" people, plus in high school and when Linda and I first got married, I worked for Western Sheet Metal (owned by Stuart O'Neal) in San Angelo. I really enjoyed the work there and the men I worked with, so it was some good years and memories for me.

Anyway, after the murder investigation was finished and forgotten about, I still kept in contact with Bobby and Carolyn. My wife and I visited them on numerous occasions over the next several years.

Bobby and Carolyn's daughter, Karen Overstreet, became a police officer in Petersburg, Texas. I knew her and was aware she was in Petersburg, but then I heard she ended up quitting the police department and had moved back to Lubbock.

On April 5, 1989, Bobby called and asked me if I knew anything about Karen's present situation. I told him I did not.

Bobby told me that Karen had been dating a man from Lubbock named Danny Laseman. In the early morning hours of March 27, 1989, Karen and Laseman were returning to downtown Lubbock from a dance in the south part of the city. They were traveling in Laseman's vehicle and evidently cut a vehicle off in traffic. The vehicle had followed them for awhile. It turned off on a side street, but appeared again beside Karen and her boyfriend at the intersection of 19th and Avenue Q. Laseman turned left on 19th Street. The other vehicle then pulled along side the passenger side of Laseman's car and the driver of that vehicle began shooting into the vehicle Karen and Laseman were in. One bullet struck Karen in the right thigh. Another bullet hit Laseman's left calf.

Bobby asked me if I minded working on this investigation. He told me he did not think the Lubbock Police Department was doing anything on it.

Karen had reported the vehicle to the Lubbock Police Department. In the description, Karen said the vehicle was a brown and tan Ford Bronco with a covered spare tire mounted on the rear tailgate. The spare tire cover had a white Bronco emblem on it. She said at the start of the incident, both vehicles were traveling north on Avenue Q and there were four Hispanic males in the Bronco. The Bronco turned right, or east onto 22nd Street, and, in just a matter of minutes, it had pulled back up beside them, but only the driver occupied the Bronco.

Two days after Bobby's call, shortly after lunch, I went to the Lubbock Police Department and talked with two detectives about the shooting. I was basically told there were numerous Ford Broncos in Lubbock that fit the description Karen had given and without more information than they had, there was not much the detectives could do.

The detectives said several .45 automatic cartridge cases were recovered at the scene of the shooting and were in the Lubbock Police Department's evidence room. I asked if they minded if I took a look at the case and they seemed to welcome the help, so I got a copy of the reports on file and left the police department.

I drove directly from the police department, located in downtown Lubbock, south on Avenue P. As I got to the intersection of Avenue P and 22nd, I saw a brown and tan Ford Bronco was parked on the north side of 22nd in front of a residence in the northwest corner of the intersection. Two females were sitting on the porch with their feet resting on the top step, evidently talking to one another. I turned right on 22nd and noticed the spare tire cover on the Bronco just as Karen described it. I had not been gone from the police department five minutes!

I drove on down to a location at 22nd and Avenue Q and parked where I could see the Bronco. I called our office and had the secretary call the police department and tell the two detectives what I was observing. I requested they meet me where I was parked.

While I was waiting for the detectives, one of the females got in the Bronco and drove off. I got behind her and got her stopped with my red lights at about 24th and Avenue Q. The two Lubbock PD detectives arrived at the same time I was getting the Bronco stopped. A search of the driver's purse for weapons revealed a loaded .25 caliber semi-automatic pistol. She was arrested for the firearms violation and placed in the Lubbock County Jail.

Further investigation revealed the driver and her husband had been living at the Holiday Inn on Loop 289 in Lubbock but had recently moved out owing a bill. Holiday Inn management had collected items the couple left behind in the room, including drug paraphernalia and one spent .45 caliber cartridge case.

An interview of the man who owned the house located at 22nd and Avenue P, where I observed the Bronco parked, revealed he was the brother-in-law of Eduvegis Lopez, now a suspect in the shooting. The brother-in-law confirmed that on the night in question, he, along with Lopez and two others were returning from a dance in south Lubbock when the victim's vehicle did cut in front of Lopez, who was driving the Bronco. The brother-in-law stated Lopez was mad over the incident and after letting him and the others off at his house, left in the direction of 19th Street.

Analysis at the DPS lab in Austin matched the .45 cartridge case recovered from the motel to the .45 cartridge cases found at the scene of the shooting on 19th Street.

Lopez was filed on for the attempted murder of Overstreet and Laseman and I spent considerable time in the Lubbock area and around Presidio, Texas, attempting to locate and arrest Lopez. Finally, in April of 1993, four years after the shooting, I was notified that Lopez had been killed in a drug dispute in Mexico, southeast of Juarez. After seeing a photograph of Lopez on a morgue table we were satisfied he was indeed the man we were looking for.

Grandparents' Love

On December 13, 1985, I was contacted by Royce Cody and his wife, Billie, and asked to assist in a parental kidnapping investigation. Royce and Billie had been given custody of a granddaughter, Kelly, by the District Court in Lubbock. During a visitation, Kelly was kidnapped by her mother Claudette Cody. The mother immediately left the Lubbock area with Kelly.

The case was frustrating for us. Claudette and Kelly traveled to different parts of the United States and it seemed we were always just a day or two behind them.

I had entered Claudette as a wanted person in the National Crime Information Center, a data base administered by the Federal Bureau of Investigation to locate fugitives and stolen property. This case was not that difficult to work on, it was just very, very frustrating. I could see the day-to-day anguish in the faces of Royce and Billie knowing Kelly was out there somewhere, not being taken care of properly. Sightings were slow to come in and agencies we had requested assistance from seemed to be even slower with their follow up investigations.

On January 17, 1986, an officer at a soup kitchen in Las Cruces, N.M., ran an NCIC check on Claudette Cody as she stood in line to get food. The check revealed she was a wanted person out of Lubbock County and there was a pick up order for the daughter, Kelly. Claudette was taken into custody and Kelly was taken to child protective care until Royce and Billie could get there to take custody of her. My wife, Linda, and I traveled to Las Cruces the following day and returned Claudette back to the Lubbock County Jail.

On February 12, 1986, Claudette was tried and given five years deferred adjudication with intensive supervision of one year on the charge of interfering with child custody. The Cody family, including Kelly, and our family have remained close friends all the years since. Royce and Billie still live in Shallowater, in Lubbock County. Kelly, along with her husband and children, live in a town nearby.

A Very Sad Investigation in Garza County

One of the first families I met after making the Texas Rangers in 1977, was Larry and Kathy Bownds. Larry and Kathy managed the Chimney Creek Ranch in northeast Garza County. Kathy's father, H.C. Lewis, owned the ranch. H.C. lived in Lubbock.

I was around Larry a lot more than I was Kathy. Larry was a real good friend of Garza County Sheriff Jim Pippen, so I saw him most of the time at the sheriff's office in Post. A lot of the times Larry would have his young son, E. Paul, with him.

Larry was as nice a man as you would want to meet. Even though he probably had access to finances through his father-in-law, he was as down to earth as anyone I knew. Kathy was the same as Larry. They were both just good people.

It was 12 years after I met the Bownds, on July 20, 1989, Garza County Sheriff Freddie Cockrell requested my assistance on a double murder investigation at the Chimney

Creek Ranch. Kathy had found both her husband's and her father's bodies in the guest house where H.C. stayed when he spent the night at the ranch.

As I entered the living room of the guest house, I could see both Larry's and H.C.'s bodies. H.C.'s body was lying at the entrance to the hallway. Larry's body was located a few feet from H.C. behind a desk. He was slumped in a sitting position.

There was quite a bit of blood where the bodies were in the living room, but as I walked down the hallway to the room where H.C. slept, there was even more blood in the hallway and in the bedroom.

Kathy found the bodies early that morning. Their daughter was supposed to compete in a horse riding competition, and the whole family was scheduled to go watch her ride. With it nearing time for them to leave, Kathy went to see why Larry hadn't come back to the house. She checked the barns and outbuildings then went to the guest house. She couldn't get anyone to answer the door, so she went around to the bedroom where her father usually slept, looked through the window and saw all the blood. She crawled through the window and found the bodies.

I had been at the scene for several hours, taking photographs, measurements and collecting evidence. It was past midmorning and one of the deputies came into the house and asked if I had time to go outside and talk to E. Paul, who was requesting to see me. I went outside and saw one of the saddest sights I have ever seen. E. Paul was sitting on the top rail of a cedar fence with his feet resting on the next rail down. He had one of the most lost looks I've ever seen on anybody.

I walked over to him and I will never forget what he asked me. Just as polite as he could be, he asked me "Mr. Hunt, is my daddy in that house?" "Yes, he is, E. Paul," I replied. His next question was "Is he dead?" I replied, "Yes, I'm afraid he is." Then E. Paul asked. "Can I go in and see him?" I told E. Paul, no, "Not at this time." E. Paul thanked me for talking with him and that was it. I returned to inside the house to continue my investigation.

The investigation really took just a few days to wrap up. Evidently, H.C. had sold the ranch without informing Larry and Kathy. He did come down a day or two before the shooting and told them both that the ranch had sold and they had 30 days to move out and vacate the ranch.

This must have been more than Larry could take. He slipped into the house the night of the shooting. Larry shot H.C. five times with .38 caliber plus P ammunition, but the only fatal shot was Larry's last one. It went through H.C.'s chest and penetrated his heart.

After being shot five times, H.C. managed to get out of bed. He retrieved a five-shot revolver he had on a bed stand, and began chasing Larry down the hallway, shooting as he went.

When Larry got to the front door, H.C.'s fourth shot went by Larry's head and exited through a glass storm door. Larry must have decided he could not make it out the front door. He took cover behind the desk located between the storm door and the hallway entrance. As he rose up to see where

H.C. was, H.C. fired his final shot from the other side of the desk. The bullet struck Larry in the mouth and severed his spine.

The medical examiner's office and DPS lab spent lots of time putting the forensic evidence of this case together. There was no doubt where the shooting started and where it ended. Both revolvers used by Larry and H.C. were recovered with the bodies. Testing on bullets shot from both revolvers and the bullets recovered at the scene confirmed what had happened.

I'm very sorry this whole incident occurred. From early on in the investigation, there was no doubt about whom the suspect was and I would have hated to interview Larry. I am confident he would have confessed when confronted with the evidence had he survived.

Heartbreaks That Go with the Job

Once I got into the Rangers and began investigating crimes, it was inevitable that some of the cases I would be involved in would not get solved. These cases ranged from misdemeanor thefts to capital murders.

Of course, you would like to solve every offense you are involved in and bring a suspect to justice. But in some cases there are just no witnesses, physical evidence, or anything to point you in the right direction.

You have other investigations where there may be just enough information or evidence to give you an indication of who the offender is, but it's just not enough to get into the courthouse before a jury. These cases were especially hard for me. It's tough to get close, but just not be able to wrap it up.

I certainly had my share of these cases and I will relate several that, even today, really stick in my mind.

Capital Murder: Bruce Darrell Kelley

On the night of January 16, 1978, I was called to assist the Lubbock County Sheriff's Office in a capital murder investigation being conducted in western Lubbock County.

The victim had been working at a convenience store west of Lubbock and was found by a customer behind the counter near the cash register at approximately 10:30 P.M. The victim had apparently been shot numerous times. I went to South Plains Funeral Home to witness the autopsy while other officers stayed at the scene to try and develop leads and witnesses. Company officials determined approximately $97 was missing from the cash register.

The Lubbock County Sheriff's Office and I spent months and months of investigative efforts and never developed any leads. It is still an unsolved case.

Capital Murder: Veronica Taylor

Veronica Taylor lived in an apartment complex in east Lubbock with her brothers, sisters, mother, and grandmother. She was abducted from her apartment on the evening of March 26, 1987, and was taken to an area just north of Idalou, Texas, where her assailant raped then beat her about the head until she was dead. The Lubbock County Sheriff's Office and I were developing the investigation and we were very close to interviewing a suspect, who possibly was very violent. We felt we did have enough evidence to question him. It was about the middle of the week, and my captain, Charlie Moore, called me to the office and asked me where I was on my Fair Standards Labor Act hours. Some government worker up in a northwestern state seems to have sued his employer for not receiving paid overtime and the government was, in fact, reviewing overtime payment to all public entities.

Prior to this uproar, DPS personnel and especially Rangers were immune from having to count hours. We just worked as long as we needed and then took off. We didn't worry about overtime pay.

Anyway I was not to work a total of more than 161 actual hours in any pay period without receiving paid overtime. At noon on that Wednesday I was at my allotted 161 hours, and I still had the rest of that week plus all the next week to go before the next pay period became effective. Capt. Moore ordered me to go home and not to work any hours for a week and a half because the department did not have funds to pay us overtime.

I could not donate my time. I could not ride with the sheriff's deputies, or in any way have an expense to the DPS because the captain was worried my doing so would circumvent rules already in place by the Federal Government.

I sat at my house for the next week and a half. The Sheriff's Office interviewed our suspect and did not get a confession. I'm not sure I would have been of any value assisting in the interview, but we will never know.

Capital Murder: Mary Sinor

About 2:30 P.M. on Friday December 1, 1989, I was called by Crosby County Sheriff Red Riley who requested my help investigating a murder that had just occurred in Crosbyton, Texas.

I traveled to Crosbyton and met Sheriff Riley at the scene of the murder, a convenience store located at the intersection of Main Street and U.S. Highway 82.

The only working clerk, Mary Sinor, was lying face down behind the counter in the cash register area, dead from an apparent wound to the head.

A customer, Royce Smith, found the victim after he could not get a response over the gas pump intercom to turn on the pump. Crosbyton Police Chief Norman Luker received the call and arrived at the store at 1:55 P.M.

Smith had observed a green pickup truck occupied by two men he did not recognize leaving the store parking lot, heading east on U.S. Highway 82 about the time he was pulling into the parking lot. Chief Luker had a description of the pickup broadcast throughout Region 5 as an attempt to locate it.

The tape recovered from the cash register was our best probable source of time sequences prior to the crime. The last recorded time on the tape was 1:32 P.M. and was coded for just a few cents, indicating a purchase of some candy or gum. Just seconds before this purchase was a purchase for a quart of oil for $1.49. A check of the oil display area showed only one brand of oil sold for $1.49, that being Fina 10W-40. There were still two quarts of oil on the shelf, undisturbed.

Chief Luker found an empty Fina 10W-40 quart oil container on the west side of the building, about halfway between the front and back of the building, when he did a walk-around.

The store owner from Lubbock related that recently an ex-employee of the store who was possibly a boyfriend to the victim had written an insufficient fund check to the store. The victim had filed with the county attorney to try and collect the money, but the owner did not know the status of that filing.

The day following the murder, the Crosby County Sheriff's Office received a telephone call from a lady who lived in Seymour, Texas, who stated she had bought items and had seen the clerk alive as she and her children were leaving the store. This witness had paid for the items at 1:27 P.M., according to the cash register tape. As the witness left the parking lot, she noticed a bone-colored pickup parked on the west side of the building with two black males standing near the pickup, the same area where Chief Luker found the oil container. All photographs were taken, several latent finger prints were lifted, and numerous items that could be listed as evidence were collected and preserved on the night of the murder. The plastic oil container found outside the building as well as two full ones from inside the store were also taken as evidence. Ranger Leo Hickman stopped the green pickup Mr. Smith had seen in Guthrie and returned the two men to Crosbyton to be interviewed. It did not appear they had anything to do with the murder/robbery.

Over the next several days, more witnesses were interviewed and their statements taken. Attempts to develop leads on the bone-colored pickup and its two occupants were unsuccessful. The ex-employee/boyfriend had an alibi for the time around the shooting and nothing further could be developed on him. The lab analysis of the evidence submitted also proved negative. A complete audit of the store revealed no money was missing as a result of the apparent robbery attempt.

Leads and evidence continued to be checked for months to no avail. This murder is still unsolved.

Missing Person: Edna Blodgett

Edna Blodgett was a lady who lived by herself in Post, Texas, in the early 1990s. The best I remember, Edna was in her 60s and befriending a man about 10 years younger than her by the name of Jerry Smith. Smith and Blodgett had been seeing each other off and on for about 10 years and many people who knew them described their relationship as not too good. In July of 1993, I got a call from Garza County Sheriff Kenny Ratke who asked me if I might lend some help on a missing person investigation they were conducting. Sheriff Ratke said Blodgett had been reported missing by her mother and that Smith was suspect for doing something to Blodgett, but that no progress was being made on the case. I agreed to help some on the investigation, but I was in the process of trying to get things ready to transfer with the Rangers to San Angelo.

As we got into the investigation, I do remember how uncooperative Smith was and of his total denial of having anything to do with Blodgett's disappearance. Weeks into the investigation, it was determined Smith cashed one of the victim's checks locally after Blodgett had been reported missing. The check was for around $100, and made payable to Smith. Also, several people came forward after Blodgett's disappearance and told us Smith was talking about the many oil well shafts there were from Post to Arkansas that would be perfect place to hide a dead body. Smith told several people that if a body was placed in one of those shafts, it would never be found. When we questioned Smith, he agreeably acknowledged he had written the check and had signed Blodgett's name to it. He said he used the money to take a trip to Arkansas.

Smith was in fact indicted and prosecuted for the forgery. He pled guilty to the charge and was sentenced to several years in the penitentiary for that offense. I am sure he is out of the pen by now. Many people were interviewed as possible witnesses and a lot of country north and east of Post was searched, not only by officers but by volunteers and body locating dogs, but to this day, there is absolutely nothing to indicate what happened to Edna.

Some Things Just Can't Be Explained

I can't say I ever worked another case just like this one, although I have probably heard of some. The investigation turned out to be the most blatant case of theft by a public official I ever worked. I have not encountered another investigation in my career where so many official documents were purposely altered. How the citizens of Kent County could accept the scope and size of the theft and falsification of public records defies any logic I have. To this day, I cannot understand the reasoning behind the attitudes of the majority of the citizens in Kent County when everything came to light.

I am going to try to be as accurate as I can be, but since about the only written records I have are some personal notes and weekly reports, most of the information is from memory. There was a trial as a result of this investigation and there was a ton of evidence that was submitted to the court, so all of that would be public record.

My investigation began in May of 1988, after my captain, Bruce Casteel, requested I contact Haskell County District Attorney John Fouts and former Kent County Deputy Sheriff Charles Alderman regarding an investigation already underway.

Texas Ranger Marshall Brown, who was stationed in Haskell at the time, and I interviewed Charles Alderman at Fouts' office in Haskell. Talking with a man he had given a ticket to earlier, Charles discovered the man had paid a different fine than had been reported on the final case disposition by Justice of the Peace Lewie Jean Hilton. The man told Charles he had paid one amount and I believe the case disposition showed the fine had been suspended.

Charles checked the official docket book in Hilton's office and discovered that the name corresponding to the docket number in the book did not match the name of the man Charles had given the ticket to. "White out" correction fluid had been used in the book and another name had been inserted in that docket number.

This in itself was not earth-shattering. Hilton could have made an entry mistake and corrected it, but Charles noticed there were many more such corrections. All of them had been made using white out correction fluid.

Charles discussed what he found with the county's State Game Warden and as the warden began to check his dispositions a little closer, he thought there may be some discrepancies in the disposition reporting by Hilton.

Now, in addition to that, District Attorney Fouts stated he had been in contact with the State Judicial Commission and requested the commission ask for some records from Hilton's office. The records the Judicial Commission received from Hilton had also been altered. With all of the information Marshall and I had, we began one of the largest theft and altered document cases I have ever known of.

A book could be written on this investigation, but with that being said, I am shortening the narrative considerably but giving enough details for the reader to get some perspective of the depth of the theft.

Our investigation covered a two-year period and we gathered evidence that covered a three-year period of theft and altered documents. We gathered records from just about all of the law enforcement agencies that worked and filed cases in Kent County Justice of the Peace court. Doing so required many hours of locating officers who either had been stationed in or near Kent County, or who were currently stationed there. We spent many more hours retrieving subpoenaed information and records from the bank in Jayton and other offices.

In a nutshell, Hilton was stealing just about all money he collected for Kent County through his JP office.

Seeking explanations to certain things, we interviewed Hilton several times throughout the investigation, but Hilton's answer to just about every question was that he was uneducated and he didn't really understand numbers all that well to be able to explain the discrepancies. He would also use the same excuse in answering questions from the Kent County auditor.

The routine was this: Defendants would be issued citations by law enforcement officers working in the county. In most cases, the defendant would plead guilty to the offense and be assessed a fine by Hilton. The offense would be entered into a docket book and assigned a case number. Hilton would then use this number to report his disposition to the officer.

If Hilton collected cash money for the fine, he simply folded up the money and put it in his pocket.

If the defendant paid the fine by check, Hilton had the inconvenience of having to endorse the check Justice Peace Hilton, walk across the street from the courthouse to the bank and cash the check. Then, he would simply fold the money up and put it in his pocket.

After the disposition was made, Hilton would "white out" the entries in the docket book and enter a new case in the same spot. The process would then be repeated.

According to the Kent County auditor, Hilton had been told for years the law required him to submit an audit report to the auditor reporting the collecting and dispersal of funds through his office. For the most part, Hilton just ignored the request. He very seldom submitted any kind of report, or, if he did, the report would be very vague.

The Kent County auditor told me she had tried to get Hilton to submit quarterly audit reports and she said he did submit reports for a few quarters after that, but nothing on a regular basis. I viewed the file of audit reports she had submitted and signed by Hilton, but each report stated no fines or monies had been collected by his JP office the previous quarter.

Finally, this case went to trial in Kent County. The best I remember, it took a short while to pick and seat a jury.

Testimony lasted for several days with lots of evidence submitted for the jury's examination. After both sides rested their presentations, the case went to the jury and it took the jury very little time to find Hilton not guilty.

Justice was served to some degree however. The State Judicial Commission removed Hilton from office and he never served again as a Justice of the Peace.

I'm not sure if how much money Hilton stole from Kent County was ever established, but it had to be a considerable amount.

Welcome Home!

This, reader, is your lucky day. You're gonna get two stories for the price of one.

When working as a Ranger in Lubbock, our family actually lived in the small town of Shallowater. There was a man in Shallowater by the name of Dalton Potter. I would say Dalton was as well thought of as anybody in the Lubbock area. He owned and operated a small pig farm north of town and he also owned and operated "Pot Luck" Barber Shop and Laundry in Shallowater. Over the years we lived there, Dalton's Barber Shop and Laundry were burglarized several times. Of course, I was one of the first people Dalton would call anytime a burglary happened.

Sometime early in the winter of 1984, Dalton again had his barber shop broken into and the coin operated machines in his laundry were busted open and the money was taken. The thief also took the Coke machine that had been in the laundry. About a week later, the Coke machine was found in a caliche pit west of Shallowater, busted open with the coin box missing. About a day after the burglary occurred, a young boy, about 8 years old, who lived in a trailer house up behind the barber shop came into the barber shop and he had several Canadian coins. The boy tried the coins in the new Coke machine and they would not work. He brought the coins over to Potter and asked him if he could trade the Canadian coins for coins that would work in the machine. Potter asked the boy where he had gotten the coins and the boy answered they were from his brother.

Potter traded for the coins and then called me. He told me he was sure those Canadian coins were his and had been taken in the burglary of the barber shop. Potter went on to give me a little of the boy's family history. He said the boy's brother had just gotten back to Shallowater from Arizona, where he had been in the state penitentiary for theft or burglary, and he had just been released from prison a few days before the burglary. Potter believed the older brother had committed the burglary and had given the Canadian coins to his smaller brother. He thought it would be a good idea if I talked to the older brother. I was already in Shallowater, so I drove up to the family's trailer and knocked on the door. The older brother was home and I told him that I would like to talk about the burglaries at the barber shop and laundry a couple of nights before. I asked the brother if he would accompany me to the Shallowater Police Department for the interview. Now on occasion, I have been able to talk to suspects when I had little or no evidence and ended up getting confessions from them. Such was not going to be the case with this interview.

The interview started off pleasant enough, just normal type conversation to put the person at ease. We progressed to the point where his little brother had showed up at the barber shop a day after the burglary with the Canadian coins and he had told Potter that he had gotten the coins from his brother. The brother acknowledged giving the coins to his little brother but said they had not come from a burglary. I told him I realized there were many Canadian coins in this country, but I thought it was a little ironic that a burglary had occurred in which Canadian coins had been taken and that his brother shows up the following day at the scene of the burglary with some Canadian coins.

Well, things started to go down hill from there and the brother would not admit to any involvement in the burglary. After a couple of hours of the interview, I had absolutely no evidence or reason to hold the brother any longer, so I took him home. I told Potter no progress had been made with the investigation as a result of the interview. A couple of days later, Potter called me to say he had heard that the older brother had moved back to Arizona, the day after our interview. More investigation was done on Potter's burglaries, but no other suspects were developed.

About the same time, in the mid-1980s, a really bad actor by the name of Donnie Mack McCullar lived in Lubbock. We looked at Donnie on several serious felonies but were never able to get him filed on.

In the early spring of 1985 Donnie Mack came to San Angelo and went out to the Spring Creek/Dove Creek community to confront an associate over a drug deal—or best

I can remember, it was a drug deal. Donnie Mack ended up shooting and killing "the associate." As Donnie Mack tried to flee the associate's house, he drove up to a locked gate. As he was trying to force the lock open on the gate, the land owner drove up and Donnie Mack killed him also. Donnie Mack was arrested and taken into custody to the Tom Green County Jail.

At the time all of this happened, I was working with the sheriff's office in Lubbock on a big arson case and Donnie Mack was our suspect. I called the Tom Green County Sheriff's Office and realized they had a very strong case against Donnie Mack in Tom Green County. I went to Dean Bohannon, the captain of investigations with the Lubbock County Sheriff's Office and told him I thought we ought to travel to San Angelo and interview Donnie Mack about his activities in the Lubbock area. Any cases we could make as a result could be offered up to run concurrently with any time Donnie Mack got from Tom Green County.

Our district attorney agreed. So Dean and I traveled to San Angelo to interview Donnie Mack. We told him we would get his time for these crimes to run concurrent with the time he got in Tom Green County and he agreed to help us. We were able to clear up several things in the Lubbock area, including the arson.

As we got up to leave, Donnie said, "Oh yeah, there was one more burglary in Lubbock." He said several months ago he broke into the barber shop and laundry in Shallowater. He even told us about taking the Coke machine from the barber shop to the caliche pit west of town before breaking it open.

95

I remember saying to Donnie, "Dang Donnie, you were getting awfully close to my house when you burglarized the barber and laundry in Shallowater." He looked at me with a little grin and said, "I know, your car was parked in front of your house that night."

Get Your Own Dope

This case occurred on Christmas Day of 1990, in Kent County. I tell this story just to reveal how some people feel about the holiday season and the celebration of the birth of Christ.

I was at home on Christmas day and got a call from the Kent County Sheriff Olan Chaney. He asked me if I could meet three medevac helicopters coming into the Texas Tech Health Science Center. There were gunshot victims in the choppers. According to Sheriff Chaney a family of four who lived in the Redbud community had gotten into an argument as to how the daily ration of marijuana was to be divided.

The family consisted of the mother, Dona Daugherty, her daughter, Dolly Goolsby, a son, Devon Daugherty, and a son-in-law, Earl Johnson Goolsby. Evidently, the son-in-law had become aggravated over the way the marijuana was being divided. As a result, he shot the mother-in-law in the head with a .38 caliber revolver pistol. Next, he shot his wife in the head and then he shot his brother-in-law in the head—all with the same .38 caliber pistol. The son-in-law was in custody in Kent County, Sheriff Chaney said.

I met the helicopters at the Texas Tech Health Science Center and stayed most of the afternoon as medical personnel worked on the three victims. The mother's condition was the gravest. Next, was the daughter and the son's condition was the third worst. The daughter still had some ability to move her arms and legs although her wounds were very serious. The brother was luckiest of them all. Somehow the bullet passed front to back through his skull but barely touched the brain. It's been many years, but the last I heard, the mother was is in a vegetative state in a nursing home. The daughter had recovered with some paralysis and speech impediment and the brother almost totally recovered without any impairment from his wounds.

I really do not remember the final outcome of the court proceedings, but I heard some years later, Earl Goolsby received a 45-year year prison sentence for the shootings.

How Quick Things Can Change

On the morning of June 18, 1992, I was sitting in the coffee break room enjoying a cup of coffee with some fellow employees. Ranger Warren Yeager was there talking about a "Go-kart" motor he had seen advertised on sale in a local magazine.

Yeager's boy was in need of a motor and Yeager asked me if I wanted to ride to Wolfforth with him to look at the motor. I said, "Sure."

We went in Yeager's car and were exiting the loop at Gene Messer Ford dealership in Lubbock when a voice came over Yeager's Lubbock Police radio screaming, "Officer down, shots fired!"

As it happened, we were less than a block from the reported location, an area that contained many small apartments, and we pulled into the lot at about the same time a Lubbock Police Department car arrived. Three policemen, including Sgt. K.D. Fowler, were already at the apartments. They had been called to the apartments several minutes earlier to investigate a shooting, and upon arrival, found a dead male outside one of the apartments. The officers called for crime units and detectives and started securing the crime scene area. Someone opened the door of the apartment opposite from where the victim was lying and shot and killed Sgt. Fowler.

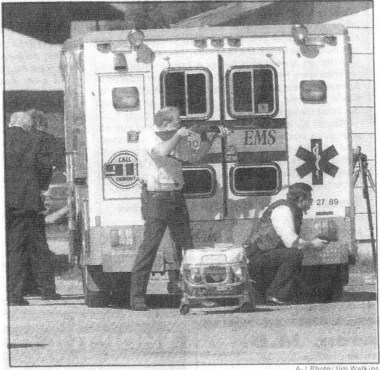

Lubbock Avalanche-Journal Fri 6/19/92

A-J Photo/Jim Watkins

Gunman at bay

Texas Ranger Joe Hunt, aiming a rifle, and police Lt. Claude Jones, kneeling, cover an apartment where police Sgt. Kenneth D. Fowler and MHMR worker James Haliburton Jr. were slain Thursday. James Kevin Voyles, 35, surrendered shortly after 11:30 a.m. to SWAT team members and was charged with murder and capital murder.

Lubbock Police Department Sergeant K. D. Fowler Murder
June 1992

We surmised which apartment the shots had come from and sure enough, someone inside the apartment began firing through the walls. Officers surrounded the apartment while the Lubbock SWAT team assembled. Then, before the SWAT team could activate a plan of entry, a male suspect exited the house and was arrested.

The first victim was a mental health caseworker who had returned to pick up the suspect and transport him to the hospital for a medical evaluation appointment. The suspect shot the case worker, then shot Sgt. Fowler as he conducted his investigation. Sgt. Fowler was close to retirement, and that was a sad, sad deal.

The Missing Fireman

"Hello Dad. Have you heard about the fireman that is missing?"

That is how the telephone conversation started between my son Mark and me, Sunday evening, April 12, 1998. That telephone conversation was also the start of what would be the last capital murder investigation I would be involved with as a Texas Ranger. It had been more than 31 years since I began my law enforcement career with the Texas Department of Public Safety.

Nemecio Nandin, a San Angelo fireman who had a side business as a washer/dryer repairman, had been reported missing by family members and a girlfriend on Wednesday April 8, 1998.

After Mark's and my phone conversation, I called the missing man's sister, Alma Camarillo. I talked with Alma for a little bit and agreed with her that it sounded as though her brother could possibly be the victim of foul play. We decided to meet the next morning at a building Nemecio had leased to do the washer and dryer repairs.

I called the DPS Special Crimes Investigator David Jones and relayed to him the information I had gotten from Alma. I told David I was going to start an investigation and invited him to assist with that. David said he would meet me at the repair shop the next morning.

David and I did meet with Nemecio's family members at the leased building. They related that Nemecio had recently been seeing a Dawn Ramirez, and Dawn had told them her ex-husband, Luis Ramirez, had threatened to kill Nemecio.

In a telephone interview Dawn repeated she felt very strongly Luis had, in fact, killed Nemecio. She stated that Ramirez's past actions left no doubt in her mind that Ramirez was the cause of Nemecio's disappearance.

We interviewed Luis Ramirez, who worked as a salesman for Jim Walter Homes. He denied having threatened Nemecio or having anything to do with his disappearance. Luis stated on the day Nemecio went missing he was in Brady, Texas, with his girlfriend, Ginger Herring. We interviewed Ginger and she confirmed Luis's statement that he and she were in Brady that Wednesday. We also got written statements from both Luis Ramirez and Herring that detailed their activities on April 8, 1998, and the time sequences of when those activities occurred.

Both Ramirez' and Herring's written statements swore to their being in a convenience store in Eden early in the afternoon of April 8. 1998. They were on their way to Brady, and then again, later, when they were returning to San Angelo from Brady. The security cameras at the Eden convenience store were checked later and clearly showed Ramirez and Herring were in the store at much later times than their sworn statements said they were.

On the morning Nemecio went missing, he had gone by his friend Greg Aguilar's house for a visit. Greg was also an appliance repair technician and was teaching Nemecio the trade. We interviewed Aguilar who stated Nemecio did come by his shop that morning. Aguilar said Nemecio told him he had "nothing going on." The two visited a short while, and then Nemecio left. Aguilar also said that about an hour after Nemecio left his shop, he called Aguilar back and said he had received a request to go to a ranch near Miles, which is about 19 miles east of San Angelo, and fix a washer. Nemecio seemed excited about the request because the person requesting the service had offered to pay an $85 service call fee. According to Aguilar the usual service fee was $60 to $65 a call.

Aguilar said he told Nemecio he probably had the parts on hand at his shop to fix the washer and invited him to come back by and get them before going to Miles, but he said Nemecio didn't stop back by and he did not speak to Nemecio again after that phone call.

We subpoenaed all the phone records for Nemecio's shop, home and cell phone. When we received the results of the cell phone subpoena it revealed a call to Miles shortly after noon on Wednesday, April 8, 1998. The phone number in Miles was registered to Richard Riordan.

Several days passed and we were following other leads as to possible suspects. On April 16, 1998, we were at the Tom Green County Sheriff's Office interviewing a deputy about some information he had when the call came in from a woman named Lana Riordan who had found a body buried on their property near Tennyson, between San Angelo and Miles.

After arriving at the scene, we were able to identify the body as Nemecio Nandin's from the description of clothing. Then, as we interviewed Mrs. Riordan, it did not take any time to determine there was a man living with her and her husband who had ties to Jim Walter Homes. A little further investigation connected the man, Edward Bell, to Luis Ramirez.

With the background work David and I had already done on Ramirez, things really began to fall into place. Different people were interviewed by various officers that evening. David and I interviewed Richard and Lana Riordan. They really tied Bell to Ramirez together as being close associates.

Texas Ranger Jerry Byrne interviewed a man whose last name was Hoogstra, a friend of Bell's. Hoogstra had in his possession a pair of handcuffs, which Ranger Byrne took in as evidence. He told Byrne he had been given the handcuffs by Bell and Bell had told him the handcuffs were used to secure the victim just prior to shooting him. Hoogstra said Bell also told him the handcuffs had belonged to Luis Ramirez.

With the information we gathered that evening and night, we were able to obtain capital murder warrants for Ramirez and Bell. Early the next morning, April 17, 1998, we arrested Ramirez at his residence, but efforts to locate Bell were unsuccessful. During our search for Bell, we determined he had left San Angelo the previous morning with his girlfriend, Lisa McDowell, to go to Tyler to work on a construction job with a friend of his.

The same day we arrested Ramirez, I called Texas Ranger Ronnie Griffith in Longview and requested his assistance in attempting to locate Bell. On Sunday morning, April 19, 1998, I received a call from a man with the information that his daughter and Lisa McDowell had just left the Walmart store in Whitehouse, Texas. The man said he had been told Bell and the man's two sons were working at a construction site that morning.

Sgt. Jones called DPS Special Crimes Sgt. Jack Allen in Tyler and requested Allen go to the construction site and attempt to locate Bell. I also called Ranger Griffith and asked him to travel to Tyler to assist Sgt. Allen. Sgt. Jones and I left San Angelo and headed for Tyler to assist in the search and while we were on the way, we got a call from Sgt. Allen saying they, in fact, had Bell in custody.

When we arrived in Tyler, Sgt. Allen told us Bell had requested an attorney and would not be interviewed. Sgt. Allen and Ranger Griffith had already contacted McDowell and gotten her consent to search her vehicle which Bell had been driving. Bell's wallet was found in the vehicle.

Two business cards from Luis Ramirez, Jim Walter Homes, were found in Bell's wallet, along with a hand-drawn map with directions and addresses to Dawn Ramirez's home and to her uncle's home in Austin.

We returned Bell to San Angelo and released him to the Tom Green County Sheriff's Office. Lisa McDowell followed us back from Tyler to San Angelo. She went to her aunt's house to stay. The next day we had another interview with McDowell and she told us on the day Nemecio was killed, Bell had followed Ramirez back to San Angelo in Nemecio's pickup and parked it behind the Walmart in north San Angelo. Then she said Ramirez dropped Bell off at her aunt's house and she drove Bell to the Riordans' house so Bell could get some personal things. McDowell said on the way Bell threw two items out of the passenger window of the car. She thought both items were rubber gloves.

Jones and I took McDowell to the location where Bell had supposedly thrown the two items out of her car. Almost immediately we found one rubber glove. We weren't having much success finding the second glove, but, I found a set of keys on a key ring lying in the grass. We photographed the glove and keys where we found them, then collected them so they could be preserved as evidence. After returning to San Angelo, we tried the key we found in the bar ditch in Nemecio's pickup ignition switch. The pickup started right up.

I retired before Ramirez went to trial, but he was tried on the capital murder charge, found guilty and sentenced to death. I did testify and present evidence at Ramirez's trial. Luis Ramirez was executed at Texas Department of Correction on Oct. 20, 2005. I don't remember if Bell pled guilty or was tried on his murder charge, but I know the state did not seek the death penalty. Bell is serving a life sentence in the Texas Department of Corrections.

There is one side story to this investigation I found humorous. Gathering evidence for the prosecution of this case required I go to Las Vegas, Nev., to confirm or verify certain facts. A critical part of the investigation included tying the handcuffs that were used to restrain Nandin during the murder to Luis Ramirez.

There was no serial number found on the cuffs, but we were able to uncover other vital records. Luis Ramirez had gone to work as a part-time security guard in Las Vegas. The records showed Luis had purchased a pair of similar cuffs and paid for them with a personal check the day he went to work there. In order to secure these records, Las Vegas Homicide Detective Dave Mesinar and I were required to appear in person at the casino security office where Ramirez had gone to work. We called ahead to make arrangements to meet with security personnel at the casino.

We went to the security office in the lobby of the main casino and informed the guard who we were and why we were there. He stated he knew we would be coming and asked to see our identification credentials. Satisfied our identifications were in order, he called another security office and informed them we had arrived.

In a few minutes, an elevator opened and another security guard greeted us. He also asked to see our identification, and once satisfied, requested we follow him. We got on the elevator and went down at least one floor. This guard told us he was taking us to the security office to meet the head of security.

We walked for a good ways, going through two or three more locked doors on the way. Each door had its own security guard. Each guard asked to see our identification cards.

We finally got to the security office and were asked by the receptionist to have a seat. The security director would be there shortly, she said.

We had been sitting there maybe two or three minutes when the door to the office opened from the hall.

In walked a pretty rough-looking young man holding about eight or ten helium-filled balloons, all different colors.

The receptionist jumped and pushed her chair back from her desk. She asked the guy in a kind of a loud voice what he was doing there. He replied he had been paid to deliver the balloons to Mr. Smith's office for his birthday. He then asked for directions to Smith's office.

The receptionist asked the man how he had gotten into the security area. He replied he had walked through the delivery doors located at the loading dock and just "walked down here."

The receptionist had activated some security button as the man first entered the room and by the time she had asked him her few questions, two armed security guards came into the room. They escorted the man away.

I looked at Detective Mesinar and grinned. I told him if we had occasion to come back to see the security director, we could just come through the delivery doors and save a lot of time showing identification cards.

San Angelo Fireman Nemecio Nandin

Show Me the Proof

All law enforcement officers over the years have had this type of suspect. The officer will have the suspicion of someone's involvement with a crime, a little circumstantial evidence, or maybe just a hunch their man is the guilty party, and, for whatever reason, the officer goes ahead and confronts the suspect about his guilt.

Many times this works. The suspect will give you the evidence you need, such as a confession or a good lead to the fruits of the crime.

But every once in a while, you run up against a suspect who flat out denies knowing about a crime or being involved in it. These are the "show me the proof" types. What a satisfactory feeling it is to get that proof and go back for a second interview. You talk about attitude change.

I have had my share of these kinds of investigations and suspect interviews over the years. One was "The Roundup Robbery."

In late December of 1979, I got a call from the Lamb County Sheriff's Office asking me to meet Hockley County deputies at a small grocery store in Roundup, Texas. Two men had just robbed the small store, and, in the process of the robbery had pistol-whipped Charles Barrett, the owner of the store.

As I neared the scene, deputies put out an "attempt to locate" on a red Chevrolet Camaro, occupied by three people. According to the vehicle description, twin white CB radio antennae were mounted on the car, one on each rear fender.

Mr. Barrett said the two black males had entered his store and the smaller of the two approached the sales counter with a small bag of potato chips that he laid on the counter. The larger male then asked for a soft drink, which was kept in a cooler box behind the counter. Mr. Barrett turned his back to the pair while retrieving the soft drink and when he turned back around, the larger male struck him in the head with a pistol.

The two left the store with money from the cash drawer. They left the potato chip bag on the counter.

A farmer's wife, living just south of the store, saw the Camaro drive right in front of her house and she was able to furnish the description of the occupants and the vehicle as it fled the scene.

A few weeks later, a vehicle was located in Lubbock and the driver, identified as Mae Helen Johnson, was brought to the Lubbock DPS office and interviewed. Johnson admitted to having the vehicle on the day of the robbery but denied any involvement. Johnson stated on the day of the robbery, she had taken her brother, John E. Johnson to the parole office. She also had another brother, Bobby Ray Johnson, in custody in Lubbock County on an attempted capital murder warrant.

Both brothers were interviewed and denied any involvement or knowledge of the robbery.

I processed the potato chip bag for latent fingerprints and found two prints that were very good and identifiable. I hand carried this bag to Austin DPS Crime lab to be photographed and analyzed. The two latent prints came back as a positive hit on Bobby Ray Johnson.

When shown the letter from the DPS lab stating the latent prints on the potato chip bag were indentified as his, he gave a statement as to his involvement.

Also, Mae Helen Johnson was interviewed again and she gave a statement as to her involvement in the robbery.

John E. Johnson would not admit to being involved and could not be identified by Mr. Barrett and he was never charged with robbery.

Bobby Ray Johnson pled guilty and received 10 years in prison. Mae Helen Johnson was given probation.

After the robbery, Mr. Barrett never re-opened his store.

Another good evidence case is one I call "DNA on a Calf."

In the summer of 1992 I got a call from Jay Bird in Post, Texas. Mr. Bird raised show calves and told me he had consigned with a man in the Cross Plains area to sell one of Bird's calves. Bird said this man had stopped by his ranch in Garza County around the first of the year and in fact took three calves back to Cross Plains with him on a verbal agreement.

At the end of February of 1992 Bird said he was on his way to Houston and stopped by the man's ranch at Cross Plains. Bird said the man told him he had sold one of the calves, but that Bird was not going to like who he sold the calf to. Bird said he had told the man he didn't care who he had sold it to as long as he got the money for the calf. But then the man said he might as well tell Bird the truth. He had given the calf some worm medicine and it died. Bird said he had no way to prove or disprove this.

Some months later, Bird was attending a stock show and a man he was acquainted with came up to him and said, "I hear your calf won top honors at a show in the panhandle."

Bird made a few inquiries and said he determined the calf had to be the one he had sent to Cross Plains to the auction. Bird was able to get information that Nelson Hogg in O'Donnell, Texas, was the current owner of the calf.

Bird continued that Dawson County District Attorney Investigator Cora Brown had already done some work on getting blood samples compared on the calf that was sold to Hogg to the mother cow Bird still had, as well as on the bull's semen on file at Texas A&M. I contacted Investigator Brown and learned she had received test results showing the calf Hogg had was the calf of the cow Bird had.

Armed with the information from Investigator Brown, I contacted our suspect at Cross Plains. He maintained his story that Bird's calf had died and the calf that Hogg had actually came from "north." I asked our suspect to furnish me the name of the person he had bought the calf from, but all he would respond with was that it was from "north." I asked him if "north" was the name of a man and he said, "No I just bought the calf from up north." He would not give me a name. At first, I did not tell our suspect anything about having blood test results on the calf, but I said I was going to leave and probably present my investigation to the Garza County grand jury for them to make a decision.

Then, just as I was about to leave, I told our suspect of the blood evidence we had on the calf.

All of a sudden, our suspect wanted to talk with Mr. Bird. I agreed to give him a certain amount of time before presenting the investigation to the Grand Jury.

Within a few days, Mr. Bird had been paid for the calf. Mr. Hogg sold the calf back to the suspect and no action was sought against the suspect. All parties to the investigation were satisfied with the outcome.

That Ranger Mystique

The Texas Ranger mystique modern Texas Rangers enjoy is a reputation built and solidified by Texas Rangers of old. Today's Rangers benefit because of those lawmen doing what they did very well during a time period when law enforcement and investigations were extremely difficult. The effectiveness of those Rangers, their methods of operation and the sometimes ruthless way they enforced the law, gave the Rangers a reputation that still carries on to this day.

I can't explain why, but I have seen on more than one occasion, where local authorities have tried to resolve investigations or interview witnesses or suspects and come up empty. In some cases, the local authorities could call the Texas Ranger assigned to their area and in an interview with the Ranger the witnesses and suspects will open up and a resolution to the investigation is secured. I have been part of such cases myself.

I am proud to say the Texas Rangers' reputation has spread nationwide. As I did investigations that led to other parts of the country, I never had any problems working with local authorities. More than a few times the mention of "Texas Ranger" brought a response. Here are a couple of examples of cases I was involved in where this happened.

The first one I will call, "Let's have a look." I can't remember the year now, but I worked with Kent County Sheriff's Deputy Charles Alderman on a burglary that occurred on a ranch in that county.

Two young men from Mississippi hired on as hands at this Texas ranch. I can't remember the rancher's name, now. But the boys worked for a day or two and then decided this type work wasn't to their liking. They quit in the middle of one night, taking saddles, guns and other property with them.

There wasn't much to the investigation, we knew where they were from and had authorities on the look out for them there. Sure enough, they showed up in a few days, were taken into custody and admitted the theft. They waived extradition back to Texas. Deputy Alderman and I went to Mississippi to get them and transport them back to Kent County.

The boys had admitted in their statements they had sold or pawned most of the items taken in the theft and they had agreed to try and show us the places they had discarded the property so we could recover as much as we could.

About midafternoon on the return trip, we had gotten as far as Memphis, Tenn., and the boys stated they had sold one of the guns at a pawn shop downtown.

They directed us to the location of the pawn shop and since we had no radio communication with local authorities, we found a pay phone and I called the police department dispatcher. I told her who I was, that I was a Texas Ranger and explained our situation. I asked if the officer on duty covering the area of the pawn shop would meet us there in an effort to recover the gun. She agreed to have an officer meet us.

We went back to the pawn shop to wait. In a few minutes, police cars began to come from every direction. There were marked patrol cars and a few unmarked cars, probably 12 to 15 units showed up at our location. I asked one of the first officers to arrive if this many officers normally covered the downtown area and he said, "Oh no, everybody just wanted to see a Texas Ranger."

Another case I call, "Oh Yeah, That Money." In this incident, I helped one of our secretaries recover some money that had come up missing from their high school class reunion fund.

It seems like the custodian of those funds got a little sticky-fingered and spent the money on some personal items. When confronted about the missing money by fellow classmates, he did not deny taking the money, but he would not repay what he had stolen.

I called him, told him who I was, that I was a Texas Ranger, and said I would be opening up a theft investigation concerning the missing money.

Strangely enough, the money suddenly appeared back at the bank in the reunion fund.

*Left: Joe Hunt,
Fort Polk, La.*

*Right: Joe Hunt,
at rifle range,
Fort Polk, La.*

LAST FORMATION   DELTA BATTERY   3rd BATTALION
132 FIELD ARTILLERY   49TH ARMORED DIVISION
JAN 1968

Last formation as artillery battery, San Angelo, TX.

STATE TROOPER JOE HUNT
...Takes Position In Squad Car

Stand off with armed suspect in west Odessa

Right: Patrolmen Joe Hunt and Lynn Reese teaching gun safety in Odessa

Tomorrow's Forecast

Rain Chance

Details, Page 2A

THE ODESSA AM

A FREEDOM NEWSPAPER

Vol. 52-No. 172   Odessa, Texas, Wednesday, June 22, 1977

Grinding crash kills father and daughter

Harold Hayes of Hanover, Pa., and his 16-year-old daughter, Karen, were killed instantly today. Mrs. Hayes and her 18-year-old daughter, Elaine, were hospitalized and three other members of the Hayes family escaped uninjured when their motor home slammed into a westbound moving van that was in the eastbound lane of traffic shortly before 11 a.m. today. The crash h East loop 338 and Interstate Highw related pictures, story, pages 2A.

Fatal traffic accident, IH20, Odessa

Ranger Sr. Capt. Bill Wilson at KKK rally in Austin

Drug bust in Lubbock

L-R: Ranger Joe Hunt, Sheriff Jim Pippin, DPS Trooper Louis Cardinal, Post, TX.

Ranger Lt. Carl Weathers and Ranger Sergeant Bill Gerth, Guthrie, TX.

Scene of double homicide, Lorenzo, TX.

Recovery of buried murder victim, Coke County, TX.

DEPARTMENT OF PUBLIC SAFETY

IN THE NAME AND BY THE AUTHORITY OF

The State of Texas

To All to Whom These Presents May Come -- GREETINGS:

BE IT KNOWN, that the Public Safety Commission, and the Director of the Department of Public Safety of the State of Texas, reposing special trust and full

confidence in the integrity and ability of _____ JOE BURL HUNT _____

of the city of _____ AUSTIN, TRAVIS _____ County, Texas,

do by virtue of the authority vested in us by law, constitute and appoint him a

DRIVERS LICENSE PATROLMAN

and do hereby commission him as a law enforcement officer of the Department of Public Safety of the State of Texas as authorized by Chapter 181, page 444, General Laws, Acts of Regular Session of the Forty-fourth Legislature in said State of Texas, giving and hereby granting to him all the rights, privileges, and emoluments appertaining to said appointment.

IN TESTIMONY WHEREOF, I have, with the approval of the Public Safety Commission, hereunto signed my name and caused the seal of the State of Texas, Department of Public Safety, to be affixed at the City of Austin, the ____1st____

day of _____ JUNE _____ A. D., 19 67

Age 22   Height 5' 10" Weight 165   Hair BROWN Eyes BLUE Complexion MEDIUM

(SEAL)

Director, Department of Public Safety

PUBLIC SAFETY COMMISSION

John Peace, Chairman
Garrett Morris, Member
Clifton W. Cassidy, Jr., Member

2463

Commission to Driver License Patrolman, June, 1967

DEPARTMENT OF PUBLIC SAFETY

IN THE NAME AND BY THE AUTHORITY OF
The State of Texas

To All to Whom These Presents May Come -- GREETINGS:

BE IT KNOWN, that the Public Safety Commission, and the Director of the Department of Public Safety of the State of Texas, reposing special trust and full

confidence in the integrity and ability of _____ JOE BURL HUNT _____

of the city of _____ AUSTIN, TRAVIS _____ County, Texas,

do by virtue of the authority vested in us by law, constitute and appoint him a

HIGHWAY PATROLMAN

and do hereby commission him as a law enforcement officer of the Department of Public Safety of the State of Texas as authorized by Chapter 181, page 444, General Laws, Acts of Regular Session of the Forty-fourth Legislature in said State of Texas, giving and hereby granting to him all the rights, privileges, and emoluments appertaining to said appointment.

IN TESTIMONY WHEREOF, I have, with the approval of the Public Safety Commission, hereunto signed my name and caused the seal of the State of Texas, Department of Public Safety, to be affixed at the City of Austin, the ____ 11th ____

day of _____ MAY _____ A. D., 1970

Age _25_ Height _5'10"_ Weight _170_ Hair BROWN Eyes _BLUE_ Complexion _FAIR_

Wilson E. Speir

(SEAL)

Director, Dept. of Public Safety

PUBLIC SAFETY COMMISSION

Clifton W. Cassidy, Jr., Chairman
Marion T. Key, Member
William B. Blakemore, II, Member

1192

Commission to Highway Patrolman, May, 1970

DEPARTMENT OF PUBLIC SAFETY

IN THE NAME AND BY THE AUTHORITY OF

The State of Texas

To All to Whom These Presents May Come -- GREETINGS:

BE IT KNOWN, that the Public Safety Commission, and the Director of the Department of Public Safety of the State of Texas, reposing special trust and full

confidence in the integrity and ability of_____ JOE BURL HUNT _____

of the city of_____ AUSTIN, TRAVIS _____ County, Texas,

do by virtue of the authority vested in us by law, constitute and appoint him a

TEXAS RANGER

and do hereby commission him as a law enforcement officer of the Department of Public Safety of the State of Texas as authorized by Chapter 181, page 444, General Laws, Acts of Regular Session of the Forty-fourth Legislature in said State of Texas, giving and hereby granting to him all the rights, privileges, and emoluments appertaining to said appointment.

IN TESTIMONY WHEREOF, I have, with the approval of the Public Safety Commission, hereunto signed my name and caused the seal of the State of Texas, Department of Public Safety, to be affixed at the City of Austin, the ___15th___

day of _____ JULY _____ A. D., 19 77

Age 32 Height 5' 11" Weight 190 Hair BROWN Eyes BLUE Complexion FAIR

(SEAL)

Wilson E. Speir
Director, Dept. of Public Safety

PUBLIC SAFETY COMMISSION

Ottis E. Lock, Chairman
Robert R. Shelton, Member
William B. Blakemore, II, Member

1192

Commission to Texas Ranger, July, 1977

Back row L-R: Sister Carolyn Cornelius with dog Baxter,
Eddie Cornelius with dog Beau, Corey Nelson, Kelly Nelson
Front row L-R: Carter Nelson, Cole Nelson

L-R: Wesley Hunt, Haley Hunt, Jalain Bagley, Laura Macias, Robert Hunt,
Linda (Smith) Hunt, Brother Skipper Hunt

Above L-R: John Thomas Hunt,
Brother Jerry Hunt,
Amber (Hunt) Elkins

Right: Son Bryan Hunt,
Brittny Hunt

L-R: Son Mark Hunt, Jamilyn (Lange) Hunt, Rylie Hunt, Taylor Hunt

*Left: Custom Engraved
.45 Auto with tooled
gun belt worn while
in Rangers*

*Below: Issue Highway
Patrol pistol and gun
belt, May 1970*

Original July 1977 issue identification card

Badges authorized for Joe B. Hunt during his career

Helps Keep You Out of Trouble

I am not sure that this is where this story belongs, but I guess it is as good as place to put it as any. Through the years being a Ranger got me lots of forgiveness from my captains and lieutenants. Maybe this is because as Rangers we had individual freedoms we tried not to abuse and our supervisors were a little more lenient toward our behavior on occasion. I am not sure when this particular incident occurred, but it seems like it was spring weather and it was staying light a little longer in the evening.

One half of the Ranger Service was in Austin for In-Service training for that week. One of our scheduled training days was to drive to the DPS Rifle/Tactical Range located six or eight miles out of Austin. As it turned out, this was the first time I had ever been to this range. Prior to the start of what was to be two-part training, we were all gathered together by the DPS Range Officer, Reeves Jungkind. He told us he had just spent considerable time and effort getting a "suspect vehicle" brought to the range and getting it located in the right position for the first exercise. Jungkind also told us there were no stray bullet holes in the "suspect vehicle" and by the way the suspect targets were positioned, he felt a Ranger should have more than adequate ability to be able to hit the target and manage to keep from hitting the car. I do not think Rangers were favorites of Jungkind's. He seemed really condescending in admonishing us not to shoot this vehicle.

For the first exercise, a two-man Ranger team was assigned to a vehicle and we were supposed to do a felony stop on another vehicle; get involved in a shooting with the "suspects" in the car and do it in a safe manner. The logic was to have both Rangers engage the target, but only one Ranger would engage the target at a time with pistol fire. As the first Ranger expended all of his ammunition, the second ranger would then engage the target with pistol fire enabling the first Ranger time to reload his weapon and magazine.

We were to shoot this course with each Ranger getting the opportunity to engage the targets and reload his weapon. Now about this time, the Ranger service had gotten some new night vision equipment and some scopes. So, the second part of our agenda was to stay at the range until dark and look over this new equipment and become familiar with what it could do in the dark.

Jungkind had brought the needed ammunition for both exercises in his DPS issued station wagon. There was plenty of ammunition stored in this vehicle.

We started the first exercise on the two-man felony team and probably finished somewhere in the neighborhood of around 4 P.M. Every Ranger got a turn and the exercise went

OK. When we finished the first exercise, Jungkind got our lieutenants together and said he was going home for the day. He said he was going to lock the station wagon and leave the keys with them so that after the night exercise someone could bring his station wagon back to the DPS Academy and park it. Jungkind left and shortly after he had left, our captains, who were at the range, left too. It was getting seriously close to beer drinking time and all of the supervisors were abandoning ship to leave all of us to wait for dark. One of the lieutenants had the keys to Jungkind's station wagon and he was to be back around dusk to give us our ammunition for the night exercise. This left Joaquin Jackson as the senior Ranger in charge.

It wasn't very long after all of the supervisors left that Joaquin decided he wanted to check the "zero" on his sniper rifle. Joaquin got his rifle out of his car and placed it on the top of it, and began looking for a target. This is where things went south in a hurry. The only thing Joaquin could see that suited him as a target was a chrome gas cap on Reeves Jungkind's new suspect car. Joaquin shot the gas cap several times, satisfying himself that the "zero" on his rifle was OK. About this time, Ray Martinez decided he wanted to check the "zero" on his sniper rifle. I think Ray picked a chrome door handle on the car to satisfy himself that the "zero" on his sniper rifle was also OK.

Well, this opened the gates. Before it was over, every Ranger out there had retrieved every bullet they had in their Ranger car and expended every last one of them into Jungkind's new suspect car. In addition to that, someone broke into Jungkind's station wagon and we shot all of that ammunition up in pretty short order at the car. It was still well before dark and a while before the lieutenant with Jungkind's station wagon keys was due back, but we were out of ammunition and we really didn't feel like waiting until dark just to look through a night scope. Most of us had already seen night vision equipment at police and sheriff departments in the areas where we worked anyway, so we left. I don't remember ever having any repercussions for our early departure. As for Jungkind, he got plenty mad over having his new car shot to pieces, but he got over it.

Another Reason to Love Your Lieutenant

In the DPS, when you have an automobile accident or what is called a "fleet accident" (whatever term you prefer), it generates more than the usual paperwork than what an ordinary citizen would have to fill out. Not only were there extra reports for the DPS driver to fill out, the accident caused the driver's supervisor to have to complete some reports. Therefore, if we ended up involved in a fleet accident, we could count on spending some extra time doing paperwork.

When I retired from the DPS and the Rangers in November of 1998, I chose to be paid for some unused vacation and overtime with cash money in lieu of taking the time off. Consequently, I had to work on the very last day in November. On that day, I showed up at the DPS office in my state car with thoughts of getting some last minute things done. About mid-morning on that day, my lieutenant in Midland, Joe Sanders, called me on the telephone and told me that he and the captain would like to come to San

Angelo before lunch, inventory the items I would be turning in, and get back to Midland shortly after lunch time.

I told the lieutenant that I still had some things to do and that was going to be too early and asked him if they could wait and come after lunch. I explained to him I still had a few pieces of evidence I needed to take by and release to the investigation division of the sheriff's office. I also told him I had a few reports the district attorney's office had requested on the same investigation.

Lt. Sanders agreed to wait and said he would see me after lunch. I packed up everything I needed to deliver to the sheriff's and the district attorney's offices and left my office heading downtown. On the way downtown I was going to drive right by my bank and thought I would withdraw some money just in case the lieutenant and captain wanted to eat a late lunch.

As I pulled into the parking lot in front of the bank, there was a big crew cab pickup with dark tinted windows backing out of a parking space. I stopped in the parking lot, just off of the street, to give the pickup plenty of room. However, the pickup pulled back into the same spot it had just pulled out of. I thought this was an indication the driver of the pickup wanted me to come on and get around him. I started on into the parking lot and was "at that point of no return," when the driver of the pickup backed up a second time. This time the pickup hit my car, damaging the front left fender and headlight area. It was certainly enough damage that you could see.

I immediately got on my cell phone and called my lieutenant in Midland. When he got on the phone, I said something like, "Guess what?" When he said he didn't know, I replied, "I just had a fleet accident on the throughway in San Angelo." I do remember his response. "You have got to be sh----- me," he said, to which I replied, "Not one bit." I told him that I was still headed downtown to deliver the evidence and reports; that the car was drivable and that I would do a small report on the accident. I told the lieutenant I knew I would not have time to do the full-blown report and that he would have to do it, but I knew he wouldn't mind. I remember also jokingly telling him, "If it will make you feel any better, I will give you my safe driver pen when you get here." I hate that the accident happened on my last day, but I know Lt. Sanders loved me enough to be willing to step up and take care of everything that needed to be done.

Fleet accident last day to work for DPS
San Angelo, TX., November 1998

You're Not Going to Believe This, But …

One cold snowy, icy day in Lubbock, I got a call from Sheriff Red Riley in Crosby County. Some tires stolen from a co-op in Crosby County had just been seen in an apartment beside a house in Lubbock, the sheriff told me. The house, supposedly occupied by an older man, was located on about 15th Street near downtown Lubbock.

I found the house and there was an apartment located on the east side of it, so I went to the door of the house and knocked. A man—I don't know if he was older, he was about my age at the time—answered the door. I was wearing a coat and identified myself as a Texas Ranger and showed the man my identification.

I told him the reason I was there and said I had information he had some stolen tires in the apartment. He denied having any tires in the apartment so I asked him if he minded if I went in and looked for myself.

He said he would not mind at all, but the apartment was locked and his wife had just left with the key. I said, "OK, why don't I leave you one of my cards and when she gets back, just call me, I'll come back and we can look then." He said that would be fine. He would call me the minute she returned. I gave the man my card and left.

As I drove off, I called my lieutenant at the office and asked if he could bring me the Ranger surveillance van and meet me at a parking lot just about a block north of the suspect's house. I had already parked in the lot, keeping an eye out and before the lieutenant arrived with the van, the suspect left, headed east on 15th Street in a vehicle that had been parked in a carport between his house and the apartment.

The lieutenant got there with the van, I traded him vehicles and put my camera and binoculars in the van, where I had an unobstructed view of the front area of the suspect's house.

I had not been there long at all when the suspect returned. He had a younger man riding in the front seat of the vehicle with him. He parked back underneath the carport and both men went into the house.

A couple of minutes later, both males came out of the house. The suspect male walked out to his mailbox located on the street. Now all the time he was walking, he was looking back and forth, up and down the street and the alley. After he checked the mailbox, the other younger male joined him at the alley entrance. They both were really looking around.

They walked up to the apartment and the suspect was obviously able to unlock the door. Both men were still constantly looking around in all directions. The suspect got the apartment door open and they both went inside. Within just seconds, the younger male came out with a tire under each arm. He ran to the car and put them inside. The suspect followed the younger man out with two more tires and put them in the car too. I took pictures of the whole sequence with my 35 millimeter camera.

I moved from the back of the van to the driver seat, started the van and was trying to exit the parking lot, but due to the ice, I was having trouble getting traction. In the meantime, the suspect was able to back out of his driveway and was leaving the house, westbound on 15th Street.

About three or four blocks west of the house, I finally caught up to the suspect, and, as he neared a stop sign, I pulled up along the side of his car. I had my pistol in my hand, raised it where he could see it and motioned with my other hand he pull to the right. He recognized me, indicated he understood by shaking his head up and down, pulled to the right, and stopped.

I stayed in the street and parked a little to the rear of his driver door. I was out of the van in no time and was giving him instructions to exit his vehicle. He got out of his vehicle and stood by his door. I instructed the passenger just to remain in the vehicle for the time being. I had called the Lubbock Police Department for a backup car. They were not there yet, but they were close.

The first thing the suspect said to me as he exited his vehicle was "Ranger Hunt, I know you are not going to believe this, but I was bringing you the tires." "You are right," I said. "I don't believe you." When the PD got there, we had the suspect and his friend follow us to the DPS office in their car.

Once at the office, I called Sheriff Riley and he dispatched two deputies to our office to take charge of the suspects and the tires.

Looking around for cops …

... then getting rid of stolen tires

Let's Go Hunting

I have a story about my lieutenant, Carl Weathers, and this seems about as good of a place as any to tell it. I can't begin to tell you the dates, but sometime after deer season in the mid to late 1980s, Carl asked me if I would like to go to Colorado the following year to hunt elk and deer. I politely declined, telling him it would cost way too much money for me to go. Carl replied, "No, this hunt won't be that expensive. As a matter of fact, it shouldn't cost us much at all." Carl said he had a friend down in Bay City who worked with a man who had some really nice hunting property in Colorado. Carl repeated again that I needed to go because it was going to be the hunt of a lifetime. The brother of the man Carl's friend worked for had already made arrangements for the hunt. Carl said we would be staying in a hunting lodge and pack horses would be available.

I felt for sure that staying in the lodge and having the pack horses would make the hunt too expensive for me so I told Carl I would have to go another time. Carl's friend in

Bay City was named Richard Montgomery and I believe
Coppinger was the last name of the man Richard worked
with, but I cannot remember his first name. Well, throughout the year Carl continued to talk about what a fabulous
hunt I was fixing to miss if I didn't go with them. As the time
got nearer, Carl made such a bombardment of comments
about this great hunt they were about to embark upon,
he finally got me to change my mind. The plan was for
Coppinger to come by Lubbock in the late afternoon the
day we were to leave and he would be pulling Montgomery's
jeep. Coppinger drove a nice custom Ford van. When they
got there on the afternoon, we loaded everything Carl and
I needed, including our own bedrolls to sleep in at the
hunting lodge, into the van. We took off before dark and
headed for Montrose, Colo. All Coppinger could talk about
was how fabulous this hunting lodge was, and how great the
horse pack we would be hunting off of was, and how big the
amount of game was we would be seeing, etc. and so on. We
drove all night that night and all day the next day.

The going was slow because of the road conditions, but
we finally got into Montrose about 10 or 10:30 P.M. When
we weren't too far out, however, Coppinger suggested we
make a stop before going to the lodge. "It's not midnight,"
Coppinger said, "so why don't we drive by my brother's and
my tavern in downtown Montrose and have a drink and get
a last-minute update from my brother?" I looked over at
Carl with a look that said, "This is not how I expected my
deer hunt in Colorado to start." We went on downtown,
parked, and went into the tavern. It was a fairly decent place
and Coppinger's brother was already seated at a fairly large

table in the tavern with a few other people. It was like home-coming for a family reunion. Coppinger's brother greeted everybody and was cordial enough, but after being a cop for as long as I had been, I was really uncomfortable just sitting there. Everybody but Carl and I ordered a mixed drink and it was "let the party begin." I could tell Richard was uncom-fortable too, but we really did not have any control over the situation. While the brothers talked with some others at the table, the subject came up about our deer hunt.

The brother in Colorado responded, "Well, there has been a little problem there." He said the man who was going to let us use the resort leased it just a few days ago, but, he assured us, "Everything is going to be fine." Coppinger's brother went on to explain they owned 40 acres of private land up on this mountain and he had already made arrangements with their neighbor to let us hunt on his 40 acres. Therefore, he said, we had 80 acres of some prime land to hunt on.

The brother told us he had already taken his camping trailer up to their 40 acres and he had borrowed another trailer for Carl, Richard and me to stay in. The borrowed trailer was already set up on the mountain, next to the brothers' trailer. Things were beginning to take kind of a southward look on this fabulous deer hunt of Carl's.

The next morning we got up and unhooked the Jeep from the van. It had snowed a little during the night and was still snowing lightly so the roads were what you would call "slick." After everything was ready, Coppinger and his broth-er from Colorado, his wife, and a young boy got in the van to start the journey to their 40-acre lot up on the mountain.

Richard was driving his jeep. Carl was on the passenger side and I was in the back seat as we followed the Coppingers. While it was level ground, we really didn't have much trouble with traction. As we started to climb the mountain, that changed somewhat. Coppinger's big heavy van didn't seem to be having much trouble at all but the light wheel-based Jeep was beginning to take a few slips here and there. At one point going up the road on the mountain to the tracts of land, we broke traction completely and started sliding back down the mountain. I guess you could say we really had no control over the Jeep at all. Thankfully, the Lord was with us and we slid back off the road into a berm which stopped our slide.

We got going again and it seemed like it might be snowing a little bit harder. We did make it up the mountain this time and as we pulled into the acreage where the trailers were located, I was shocked at what I saw. Coppinger's brother had, in fact, gotten their trailer up the mountain and set it up. It looked as though it was about a 30-foot self-contained trailer and appeared to be very comfortable.

The trailer sitting next to it for Richard, Carl, and me was a regular size tent trailer with no door on the entry. The two beds that were supposed to extend out each end of the trailer were still inside the trailer. Coppinger's brother told us he had borrowed this trailer from one of his buddies and that the top did not rise and beds did not actually slide out. Coppinger continued that he had raised the top up and had a 2x4 bracing each corner so that the top would not come back down. Both beds were broken so he had to just leave them inside the tarp. As I said earlier, there was no door.

There was a piece of cloth about halfway down the doorway. I guess this was supposed to break the draft coming through the trailer. There was barely room for two people to walk through the door and get to their bed at the same time. There was no heat of any type that worked.

"Hunting Lodge"

Richard was the lucky one in this ordeal. He had brought his mountain tent gear which consisted of a little one man dome tent with a separate dome tent that covered the small tent. He also had little heaters that would keep the tent fairly comfortable. Other than a pretty good size campfire outside close to our trailer, there was no other heat source available. Carl and I had identical sleeping bags and the first night there, I liked to have nearly frozen to death. We put everything as far as clothing and blankets inside our sleeping bags just to make it through the night. Thank the Lord a young man and his son hunting near us the following day took pity on us and asked us to spend the night with them on the second night. He had a really nice coal heated cabin that was very warm. The second night was really comfortable.

On the third day, Richard, Carl and I went back down the mountain to Montrose. Carl and I went to Walmart and bought sleeping bags identical to the ones we had. We spent that night in Montrose in a motel and went back up the mountain on the fourth day. We hunted another day or two without success. We stuffed the new sleeping bags inside our old sleeping bags and were at least able to get some sleep. I guess I tell you this story about Carl so that you can be aware that if anyone ever paints this picture of a fabulous hunt in Colorado, you should *beware*! At least you have been warned.

"Two Dogs" Johnson

I could certainly write a book covering the special friendships that have developed over the years. There is no way to write about every one of them, but I do want to spend some time talking about Jerry Johnson and the friendship we developed over the years.

Jerry was a man you could count on, certainly. I can't tell you how many really serious, dangerous situations we teamed up on. In every tough situation, any law enforcement officer who worked with Jerry knew they could count on Jerry to have their back. There's a picture following this writing, with Jerry and me in it. Jerry is the man at my back and we are about to enter the room where we thought Billy Wayne Alexander was. Alexander was wanted for killing DPS Trooper Jerry Don Davis the day before near Slaton, Texas.

I first met Jerry right after I made the Texas Rangers. Jerry made Motor Vehicle Theft Investigator about the same time and we both ended up being stationed at the Regional Headquarters in Lubbock.

Now, the first time I ever laid eyes on Jerry was during a two-week fingerprint school we attended in Austin. I sat next to Jerry during the school.

For two weeks, every time we took a class break, Jerry was doing something to me or my materials on the table. I would come back from break, my glasses lenses would be smeared with soap or my pencil leads would be broken. It was always something. This went on for two weeks. I spent the next 14-plus years getting even with Jerry.

Jerry was the brunt of many jokes and he brought these on by being a jokester himself. We had a lot of fun pulling things on Jerry over the years, but he had his share of fun getting back at us.

I want to relate one of our pranks we pulled on Jerry. I think it was a good one.

When Sonny Keesee took office in 1981 as Lubbock County Sheriff, he immediately asked the county commissioners for a raise for his department and for an over-sized desk chair for his office. The commissioner's court denied the raise but offered to buy the chair. Sonny refused the chair and the whole story became a big news item in the Lubbock newspaper, with Sonny at odds with the county commissioners.

The next Christmas, Sonny's employees donated money, and bought Sonny an over-sized chair for his office. This, of course, started the hoopla in the newspaper over the chair and the commissioners' unwillingness to fund raises for the sheriff's department. I was good friends with Sonny and thought it would probably be neat to steal his chair. I never gave one thought to the news media and any role they might play. But I did think of Jerry and how nice it would be to include him in this scheme without his knowledge.

DPS Polygraph Operator Ron Rodgers, Ranger Warren Yeager and I all went to the sheriff's office. The plan was for Yeager to go back to the jail, make up some kind of problem and tell the jail staff to call Sonny back there. After Sonny left his office to go back to the jail, Rodgers and I were to get the new chair from Sonny's office. Our plan was to carry the chair to the DPS office and put it in Jerry's office.

The plan went as expected. We got the chair into the Ranger surveillance van and headed toward the DPS office. However, almost immediately after leaving the sheriff's office, a broadcast came out over the police radio for local SO units to be on the look out for a green Dodge van, occupied by three white males, naming us specifically. According to the dispatch, we were suspects in stealing the sheriff's new chair.

Almost as soon as the first broadcast went out, we met a Lubbock County Sheriff's Deputy and he broadcast that he had just met the green van and it appeared to be headed toward the DPS office.

We rolled into DPS and hurriedly rolled the chair into the building and put it behind Jerry's desk. We removed Jerry's chair of course. Jerry was not in his office and he had absolutely no clue of what was going on.

Within just a few minutes, there were several Lubbock television news crews in the office and in came Sonny, wanting his chair. I told him I did not know what he was talking about, but I had seen Jerry putting a chair in his office. He demanded to see Jerry.

It would not happen again in a hundred years, but when I called Jerry on the office radio, he answered. I told him he needed to return to the office to see someone. He was out by Texas Tech, so he said it would be a few minutes before he could get back to the office. By the time Jerry arrived, most of the television stations were in the hall of the office closest to his office.

Jerry arrived at the office and as he entered and turned down the hallway headed toward his office, all the television lights came on. Sonny was standing out in front of them. He told Jerry he wanted his chair out of his office. Of course Jerry told Sonny he did not have his chair and did not know what Sonny was talking about. (It was true. Jerry had not a clue what was happening.)

Sonny asked Jerry to open his office so he could determine on his own that the chair was not in there and Jerry said, "Sure." Jerry opened his door, looked and saw the chair behind his desk and said, "Oh s---!" He quickly shut the door. Though all of this was recorded by the television crews, I don't know if they bleeped out his comment for the news broadcast or not.

But there is another little side note to the story. The Lubbock DPS office was getting a new major, starting Jan. 1 and while all this was going on, the old major was taking the new major around, showing him the office and introducing him to office personnel. I have often wondered what the new major thought of the media circus. He had to have questioned what he was getting into with his promotion and coming to Lubbock.

After it was all over, Sonny got his chair back. Jerry survived the publicity that came with the prank, no worse for wear. Jerry did tell me later that day when everything died down, that when he rounded the corner of the hall heading to his office and saw Sonny standing there, and the news media lights come on, everything he had ever done wrong flashed through his mind.

SEARCH FOR SUSPECT — Department of Public Safety officers stand with guns drawn as Texas Ranger Joe Hunt, standing nearest the door, prepares to open the door to a room at a South Lubbock motel. The DPS had received a tip that Billy Wayne Alexander Jr., 21, a suspect in the murder of DPS trooper Jerry Don Davis, was in a room at the motel. Alexander remained at large late Monday. (Staff Photo by Dennis Copeland) *Lubbock A J*

Searching for murder suspect of DPS Trooper Jerry Don Davis
L-R: Richard Addenbrook, Jerry Johnson, Tim Pringle, Joe Hunt,
Mike Humphries. Unidentified on hands and knees

The Sheriff Years

As the word got out on my pending retirement date from the DPS and Rangers, some local citizens approached me about running in the upcoming elections for Tom Green County Sheriff.

I had never been interested in running for any public office, I wanted to build and sell houses. I already had my eye on a lot out where I was living. I was going to buy it, and build our new house there.

But the more people talked to me about running for sheriff, the more I began to consider it. I finally decided to do it and began our campaigning in the fall of 1999.

We won the Republican primary in the spring of 2000 in a runoff election, and then won the general election in the fall.

I took office as Tom Green County Sheriff on Jan. 1, 2001.

I was elected to my third term in 2010 but retired after two years of that term for health reasons.

The 10 years and three months I was able to serve as Tom Green County Sheriff were the most rewarding years of my law enforcement career, including the 21 years I spent as a Texas Ranger.

To have been elected by citizens of my county to represent them as their law enforcement leader is something I will cherish until the day I die.

The employees of the Tom Green County Sheriff Office are for the most part very dedicated, professional and loyal individuals. It was my privilege to be a part of that.

With all this being said, I want to share some of the lighter times I had as sheriff.

S-T Photo by Michael Vosburg

Joe Hunt, who won the Tom Green County Sheriff's election Tuesday, looks at a plaque presented to him by supporters during his campaign victory party at the San Angelo Firefighters' lake house near Lake Nasworthy.

Joe Hunt and Linda Hunt Election night results, November 2000

Swearing in ceremony as Tom Green County Sheriff, January 01, 2001
L-R: District Judge Ben Woodward, Linda Hunt, Joe Hunt, Bryan Hunt,
Missi Hunt, Brittny Hunt, Mark Hunt

Campaigning and Results of Campaigning

During our initial campaign for Sheriff, Toad Tucker was supporting me and wanted to introduce me to some of his friends. He arranged a meeting with several men from around the county one morning at Mr. T's restaurant in San Angelo. During the meeting we went around the table and the men asked questions about my stance or position on a variety of subjects and I answered them all as best I could.

One of the men at the meeting was Wade Choate, a local rancher. It was toward the end of the meeting and I asked Mr. Choate if he had any questions for me. He replied there were two things he wanted to know. One, if I was elected, would I wear four stars on my collar? The second thing Mr. Choate asked was, "Would I keep the blankety-blank radars in them sheriff's cars?"

I immediately responded I could only comply with one of those requests. I assured Mr. Choate I would not wear four stars on my collar.

I did say, however, I would not remove the radars because I felt they were a valuable tool in a law enforcement effort in any law enforcement organization.

Mr. Choate made no response whatsoever to my answers, but at the end of the meeting, he walked up and gave me a generous campaign contribution. I took that to mean he had accepted my response to both questions and was supporting me.

After taking office, Mr. Choate called me one day, madder than an old wet hen.

It was around Christmas time and in driving out to his ranch, he was looking at some Christmas decorations a neighbor had put up. While looking at the decorations, his car veered off the road and struck a utility pole, sheering the pole in two.

Someone called the sheriff's office and our deputies responded. The deputies in turn called the Highway Patrol service to work a wreck. Mr. Choate was not happy with us calling the Highway Patrol. He felt the pole that he hit was on his property and he did not have to report the accident.

Sometime later, Mr. Choate called me again on another incident. There was a big pasture fire burning near his ranch and due to all the emergency vehicles and hoses being used to fight the fire, we had the road blocked to traffic. An alternate route to Mr. Choate's ranch was open, but it was a longer distance than he wanted to travel.

After these two instances, I wasn't sure where I stood with Mr. Choate, though I knew I liked him and wanted to keep him on my side. My brother Skipper had met Mr. Choate several times in the past, and drank coffee with him, mostly at Mr. T's restaurant.

Skipper came up with an idea to make an "unwanted" poster for Mr. Choate, and I thought it sounded good, just to test Mr. Choate's temperament. Skipper did all the work on the poster and had a couple made up. Then we arranged to meet Mr. Choate at Mr. T's restaurant for coffee.

We got to the restaurant before Mr. Choate and taped the unwanted poster up on the plate glass window at the table where we all usually sat. Several of the regular coffee drinkers joined us at the table, and then Mr. Choate arrived. As soon as he sat down, he noticed the poster. The more he read on the poster, the more he laughed and when he finished reading it, there was no doubt he liked it. We ended up having to get extra copies for him and he mailed them to several of his friends around the state.

After we unveiled the poster there was no doubt about Mr. Choate and where he stood. He had written a book titled *Swapping Cattle*. He gave me one of his books and wrote in it "To the best Sheriff we ever had. Best Wishes. Wade Choate. 2007." Copies of the "unwanted poster" and the book signature are located at the end of this chapter.

Mr. Choate passed away on New Year's Day of 2012. I sure miss the opportunity to visit with him and hear his stories.

☆**MOST UNWANTED**☆

DO NOT BE ON THE LOOK-OUT (BOLO) FOR
THIS SUSPICIOUS PERSON

WADE CHOATE

DESCRIPTION

Race/Sex	White/Male
Height	Depends on the footwear
Weight	Fluctuates with hot air expended
Eyes	Depends on degree of anger
Hair	Only his hairdresser knows for sure
Age	Depends on the century
Fingerprint Classification	Too slick for prints

RECORD

Aggravated Utility Pole Assault with a Motor Vehicle (A.U.P.A.M.V.)

CAUTION
MIGHT BE OUTSPOKEN BUT NOT DANGEROUS

Wade Choate has been identified by authorities as both a person of interest and an interesting person. He is rancher extraordinaire and possesses infamous cattle trading skills. He also known for telling unusual but creative stories that on occasion might be slightly embellished. If you have information concerning the whereabouts of Wade Choate, please DO NOT attempt to detain him or tell anyone.

REWARD

A reward IS NOT being offered or even being considered so those that do encounter Wade Choate are encouraged to ignore him or covertly look the other way.

Choate Unwanted Poster

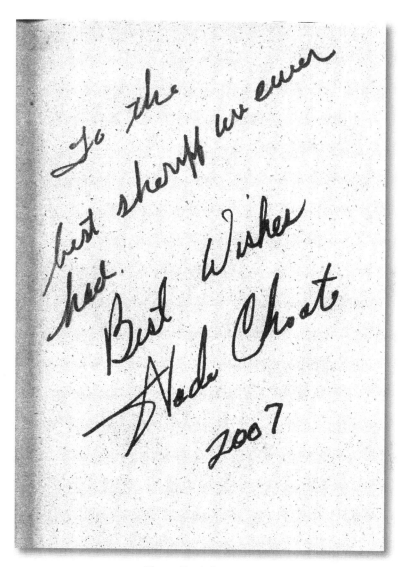

Choate Book Signature

Getting My Early Instructions
After Being Elected Sheriff

During the campaign process to get elected sheriff, there were several rumors started, I guess to try and discredit me.

One was if I was elected, I was going to fire all the current employees with the sheriff's office and hire mostly retired and current DPS employees to replace them. Another rumor was that I was for combined law enforcement and would attempt to get the police department combined with the sheriff's office.

Once elected, other county employees seemed to be a "little jittery" when dealing with me.

Just a few days after taking office, I received a call from one of the patrol deputies. The deputy said he responded to a call in the eastern part of the county. A lady's dog had reportedly been shot in her driveway by an ex-boyfriend.

The lady identified both her ex-boyfriend and the driver of their automobile, who happened to be an employee of the Tom Green County Jail.

The patrol deputy spotted the suspect vehicle, stopped it and found both suspects to apparently be under the influence of alcohol. I advised the deputy to bring them to the jail on the alcohol offense.

Very shortly thereafter, other patrol deputies discovered the suspect pair had shot up some county road and bridge equipment located just south of where the dog was shot. Then we also got a report from a farmer that two head of his livestock had been shot.

I had the jail administrator terminate our employee while he was still in custody. The next day, I received a call from Millie Wilson, the county's personnel director, and was basically told I could not fire the employee in question without going through her. She told me in the future to be sure and notify her any time, day or night, of anything concerning the hiring or termination of any employee.

I saluted, said, "Yes ma'am," and told her I could comply with her request.

A few months later, shortly after the terrorist attacks on the U.S., September 11, 2001, I was asked by the management of the San Angelo Colts semi-pro baseball team to throw out the ceremonial first pitch at the Colts' opening home game.

I got to thinking that my accepting the invitation had some potential. I called the personnel office and asked to talk to Millie Wilson. Millie's receptionist said Millie was home sick, but I told the receptionist I had a very important matter to discuss with Millie. The receptionist reluctantly gave me Millie's home telephone number.

Millie answered the phone and sounded horrible. I told her I hated to bother her at home but she had directed me to keep her abreast of any personnel matters, whatever the hour or circumstance. "That's right," she said.

Then in a very serious tone, I told Millie that today was probably going to be my last day as Tom Green County Sheriff. I expected I would be resigning the following day.

All of a sudden, Millie voice changed to normal, as though nothing was wrong with her. She asked me what I was saying and I repeated that I would probably be resigning for another job offer. "You can't resign," she said, but I told her I felt the job offer would be a significant one, and an offer I really couldn't turn down.

By that time, Millie's voice really sounded excited. She asked me if I had gotten one of the new jobs in the Federal Government dealing with Homeland Security.

I told her, "No, nothing like that." I had been asked to throw out the first pitch the following day at Colt Stadium and that after the pro scouts saw the pitch, I would surely be drafted by some pro team and be in the big leagues by the following night.

Millie used some language that even embarrassed me, but after she finished dressing me down, we both had a good laugh. At that point, I think Millie realized I did have a sense of humor after all.

How to Find a Donkey

On another occasion, I was going somewhere in town and heard our dispatcher give one of our deputies, Jock Stewart, a call to go somewhere in the county and attempt to locate a donkey or mule out on the roadway. This was not too long after I had taken office and the deputies were still a little uneasy around me.

Almost immediately after Jock acknowledged the call his sergeant, Mike Magee, came on the radio, told Jock he was near the reported location of the animal, and would come help search for it.

I got on the radio and called Mike. When he answered I told him just in case he wasn't sure what a donkey or mule looked like, they were very similar to a horse except their ears were a lot longer ears. I told him, in fact, their ears were very similar in length to his.

There was dead silence on the radio for several seconds and then the deputies' radio microphones started clicking which meant several had heard the transmission. Later I had several favorable comments from deputies, including Mike, over the "longer ears" comment. Here again, I think this demonstrated to the deputies there was a "light side" to me.

Sometimes Payback Is Sure Nice

I hadn't been Tom Green County Sheriff too long when I got a call from Texas Ranger Nick Hanna in Brownwood. Nick was at the scene of a shooting and told me they were fixing to load the victim in an air ambulance and bring him to San Angelo. He asked if one of our officers could meet the air ambulance when it arrived at the hospital in San Angelo. During the transport from Brownwood to San Angelo, however, the victim died and was pronounced dead on arrival at the hospital. Nick called me almost immediately after getting this information and wanted to know if I could be sure that a Justice of the Peace in Tom Green County would order an autopsy. I complied with his request. Shortly after the autopsy, the Tom Green County Commissioner's Court was billed for the autopsy conducted on the man from Brown County. The commissioners requested I contact Brown County Sheriff Bobby Grubbs to see if he could get their commissioners to pay the bill.

Bobby presented the agenda item to pay the bill to the Brown County Commissioner's Court and was denied because that court maintained the man died in Tom Green County and therefore, Tom Green County was responsible for the bill. When Bobby called to tell me the Brown County Commissioner's Court's decision, I kiddingly told him I didn't think that it was right, but said we would pay the autopsy bill. After that, every opportunity that I got to "rub" Bobby in any way about this bill, I did.

Well then, a letter came to me at the Tom Green County Sheriff's Office from Sheriff Grubbs. The date on the letter was April 1, 2008. In essence, Bobby's letter—which is copied along with my response at the end of this story— requested we help him recover expenses from a bonding company to the Brown County Sheriff's Office that were due. Sheriff Grubbs implied that since we had approved this particular bonding company, we were in a way liable to help him recover the expenses. His last paragraph seemed to imply that if we did more as sheriffs to hold these bonding companies accountable, it would make it easier on everyone.

In my response letter, I indicated I would be delighted to help him recover his expenses and would do so on the very day I deposited the proceeds to cover the autopsy Tom Green County had paid for Brown County. In my second paragraph I wrote that while I agreed with Sheriff Grubbs about his concern for unscrupulous bonding companies, I had my own concerns about a sheriff from one county who would send a body to another county, just to get the other county to pay for the autopsy. I called ahead to the Brown County Sheriff's Office and let Brown County Chief Deputy

Bobby Duvall know my letter was all a joke and to not let Sheriff Grubbs get too "stirred up" about it when he read it.

Brown County Sheriff's Office

Sheriff Bobby R. Grubbs
Chief Deputy Bobby Duvall
Captain Ellis Johnson

1050 W. Commerce ~ Brownwood ~ TX ~ 76801   325-646-5510 ~ 325-643-3238/Fax

April 1, 2008

Joe Hunt, Sheriff
Tom Green County Sheriff's Office
222 W. Harris
San Angelo, Texas 76903

Re: Outstanding Bill on Inmate Transport

Sir:

_____ *Bail Bonding* made a bond on an inmate in the *Tom Green County Jail* on a Brown County warrant. We billed his company for the transport cost after he was arrested in *Taylor County, Texas* and we had to pick him up on a FTA for that original charge. We have not been able to collect the cost. Since your department approved the bond, is there any way you or your Bail Bond Board, if you have one, can help us? Attached is a copy of the bill that was sent to him.

It is a concern to this agency that the bonding companies are able to make these bonds and are not accountable for our expenses incurred in handling their clients when they do not appear in court or when the bonding company has filed a surety withdrawal.

Thank you for your time.

Bobby R. Grubbs

Bobby R. Grubbs, Sheriff

Grubb's letter requesting assistance

TRUMAN RICHEY
CHIEF DEPUTY

TELEPHONE
AC 325-655-8111
FAX 325-655-5393

JOE B. HUNT
SHERIFF
TOM GREEN COUNTY
222 W. HARRIS
SAN ANGELO, TEXAS 76903

April 04, 2008

Bobby R. Grubbs, Sheriff
Brown County Sheriff's Office
1050 Commerce St.
Brownwood, TX. 76801

Dear Sheriff Grubbs,

I am in receipt of your letter dated April 01, 2008 in regards to an outstanding bill on an inmate transfer.

I would be delighted to assist you in recovery of your transport cost from **XXXXXXX** Bail Bonding Company. I will begin this recovery process for you the day I deposit the proceeds of the cost recovered for an autopsy paid for Brown County by Tom Green County.

I also agree it should be a concern of your agency as to how unscrupulous, underhanded bonding companies conduct their business. We here at the Tom Green County Sheriff's Office also share the same concern about unethical, gutter crawling, booger eating law officers that would take advantage of their fellow brothers of the cloth by sending a dead body to another county just to get the cost of an autopsy covered.

Respectfully yours,

Joe B. Hunt, Sheriff

Hunt's response letter

A Sheriff Has To Sleep When He Can

A long-time tradition in San Angelo is the rodeo, and as I found out after becoming sheriff, the San Angelo Stock Show and Rodeo Association invites local politicians and other city officials to be special guests during some of the night rodeo performances. These guests are given tickets for box seats down at the arena level. For several years, my wife and I enjoyed being seated in Box 1, seat numbers 1 and 2, right on the rail of the arena. About midway through the rodeo performances, the public address announcer, Boyd Polhamus, introduces the different politicians and dignitaries and as the different introductions are made, a spotlight illuminates the person being introduced.

Probably about three years before I retired as sheriff, we were sitting in our seats. The rodeo hadn't started yet, but the sound system during the pre-show was so loud you could not enjoy anything that was going on. I was not wearing my badge, gun or hat and I was resting my right cheek in my right hand with my index finger stuck in my ear—trying to deaden the sound.

Polhamus rides his horse around the arena during the performances and he was directly across the arena in front of me. He noticed my posture and decided, evidently, that I was asleep. About the start of the rodeo performance, I heard him say to the crowd, "Sir, you can't sleep through the rodeo performance." I had no idea he was talking to me and I sat there and kept my same posture. He then rode across the arena, stopped his horse right in front of my seat and repeated, "Sir, you can't sleep through the rodeo performance." I don't know if I responded verbally to him, but I did straighten up in my seat and Polhamus rode back across the arena to an area near the bull riding chutes.

As usual, about midway through the performances, Polhamus started introducing elected officials and I was the first introduced. Still over by the bull riding chutes, Polhamus announced to the crowd, "Tonight we have Tom Green County Sheriff Joe Hunt with us." About that time the spotlight illuminated me, and I stood to wave to the crowd. As I stood up, I heard Polhamus say over the loudspeaker, "I didn't know that you were the sheriff." I could see him galloping across the arena toward me. When he pulled his horse up in front of me and stopped, he repeated that he hadn't had any idea I was the county sheriff. "You can certainly sleep through all of this rodeo if you want to," he said. He went on to announce to the crowd he was driving the red GMC dual-wheeled pickup parked outside, when in fact his actual vehicle parked outside was a white Ford.

Later, near the end of the performance, one of the cowboys received a bad saddle bronc riding score the crowd seemed not to agree with. Polhamus rode across the arena and asked me what I thought about the score and wondered if there was anything that I could do about it.

Sometimes Experience Pays Off

I happened to be at the Walmart in west San Angelo buying some automotive parts one afternoon, and since I wasn't necessarily on duty, I was not wearing my badge or a gun. I had walked back to the automotive section and as I got to the aisle I needed to go down, there were two males and a female standing there talking and blocking the aisle. One of the males was giving the other male some cash money. The male who was getting the money had two plastic gas containers he had just taken off the shelf at the back of the store. The girl was standing there holding two or three cans of starter fluid. I stood there waiting and one of the males made some kind of comment to me—I can't remember what it was exactly, but I think it was something along the lines of, "What are you looking at old man?"

Their little trio broke up and started toward the front of the store. I thought things didn't look just right so I followed them. Their next stop was the watch battery area, and the male who had received the cash money got some lithium batteries. From experience I knew they had three of the main items they needed to manufacture methamphetamine, so, I followed them out into the parking lot. The three got into a car with a male driver and luckily, he was parked fairly close to my car, which made it pretty easy to follow them. My car was unmarked, but it did have a red and blue emergency light on the sun visor. As we headed out of the parking lot, I called to see if we had a marked sheriff's patrol unit in the area and was glad to find out we did.

I talked with the deputy and told him I felt I was following some people who were involved making methamphetamine. I followed the car as it got on the loop and the marked unit caught up with us about where Knickerbocker and the loop connect. The deputy activitated his red lights to stop the car and the car's driver attempted to evade the deputy and tried turning into a parking lot. As the deputy chased the car through the parking lot, I took the direction that would put me in front of the suspect car if it tried to re-enter Knickerbocker Road. Sure enough, we got the suspect vehicle boxed in with my car in front of the suspect car. We got all the occupants of the suspect car out to search them. The male passenger in the right rear seat had a fully loaded 9-millimeter pistol stuck in his waistband. We didn't find any other weapons in the car, but we did find some other items used to manufacture methamphetamine. All four suspects were arrested for having the paraphernalia to manufacture methamphetamine and all four had records of past drug abuse. As I was going to my car I glanced over at the suspects and asked, "Now what was that you said about an old man?"

The Lighter Side

I pride myself about all of the things I have learned to do over the years. Most of these I was taught by my dad. I've learned carpentry, plumbing, wiring and automotive repair—just to name a few of my trade skills. I am also proud of my work ethic, which is another thing my parents instilled in me. Now, this little introduction is leading up to the fact that of all the jobs I have had over the years, I have never been fired from one. Well, that is with the exception of one I had in my early days with the Highway Patrol.

When I transferred to Odessa, the Highway Patrol and Driver License offices were in a small building located on Dale Street.

Part of the lease agreement for the building was that our sergeant, O.A. Brookshire, would be responsible for hiring building maintenance workers to keep the building clean.

For a good while after I arrived, two driver license patrolmen hired out on their off-duty time to clean the building, but just like with most things, after a while, they got tired of the cleaning job and decided to quit.

My partner, Dennis Riley, and I talked it over and decided we would ask Sgt. Brookshire if we could take over the cleaning job. After all, how hard could it be to clean this small building?

Sgt. Brookshire agreed to let us do the cleaning, and Dennis and I got after it. I thought we were doing a pretty good job, but one afternoon not long after we took the job on, Sgt. Brookshire called us both in before our shift ended and "fired" us from our cleaning job. Seems there were quite a few complaints about our skills.

What a letdown to be fired as a janitor!

A Mother's Education

I was not present nor did I witness this event, but my information comes from a very reliable source, my sister Carolyn. The incident happened years ago, when the instant replay in television sports must have just come on the scene. Carolyn was visiting our mother and dad and they were all watching a pro baseball game on television.

The team Mother was rooting for was batting and the pitcher threw a pitch and hit the batter in the head, knocking him down. It took a while to tend to the injured player, and then they resumed play. But like they do with televised games, the announcers decided to show the replay of the batter being struck by the pitch when there was a lull in the game action. Mother, bless her heart, was raised on a farm near the Fairview community and went to school there. She didn't always keep up with the technology of the day, and she had certainly never seen instant replay. Mother also must have missed the announcer's commentary because she thought the video was live. Wham. That batter got hit on the head with the ball too, or so Mother thought. She let go with a tirade of how the umpires are just going to let the other team's pitcher keep hitting her team's guys in the head. Nobody was doing anything about it, etc.

After Dad and Carolyn stopped laughing, they explained to Mother the instant replay capabilities of the day.

Later that summer they were watching another game. The third baseman for the Orioles made an error and the announcers made several statements about it. Two or three innings later, the same player made another error. Carolyn and Skipper commented they couldn't believe he would make another error. But, then, the game goes on until the eighth inning. The ball is hit to third base and darn if the third baseman didn't make another error. Skipper asked Mother if she could believe that a gold glove player made three errors in one game, but she wasn't going to fall for that a second time.

"You're not going to fool me with that instant play stuff again," Mother replied politely.

A Mother's Love

While in the Rangers, stationed in Lubbock, our older son Mark attended Texas Tech University and worked 20 hours a week doing maintenance and grounds keeping duties at the DPS office.

One morning at breakfast Mark told his mother he had been betting with some bookies at Texas Tech, had lost some serious money, but he wasn't going to pay his gambling debt.

Linda told Mark he had to pay the bookies or they would find him and cause him bodily injury.

That afternoon, Mark was in the break room at DPS and told me about the conversation he had that morning with his mother concerning the bookies. He was right proud he had "pulled one over" on his mother.

I told Mark we might carry the joke a little further since she was "primed," so to speak. I talked to Ranger Warren Yeager and asked him to call me around 7 that evening, but I said once I answered he could hang up. I would carry it from there.

Usually, every night after supper, Linda and I would go back to our bedroom to watch television and that would leave Mark in the front part of the house to study or watch TV. That evening, just like we planned, Yeager called. I was at my desk working on some leather craft item. Linda was sitting up in bed, watching television and crocheting an afghan.

I answered the phone and greeted Yeager in a loud enough voice Linda would know who it was on the phone. And, like we planned, Yeager hung up and I kept talking.

The conversation went somewhat like, "No Yeager, I'm not busy in the morning. What you got? ... About 6 A.M. ... OK ... Are we gathering at DPS, Texas Tech or the police station? ... OK ... I'll be there. See you in the morning."

All the time the "conversation" was going on, I watched Linda. She never missed a stitch and every little bit, she'd look over the top of her glasses at the television. It seemed she could care less about my conversation with Yeager.

However, as soon as I hung the phone up she asked me what all that was about. I told her the Lubbock PD had requested Yeager's assistance on a raid on some bookies at Texas Tech and I was going along. She never looked my way, never missed a stitch and seemed totally unconcerned.

I got up from the desk and told her I guessed I had better get my bath and get to bed. Five A.M. would come mighty early.

When I entered the bathroom, I noticed Linda was still sitting on the bed, seemingly unconcerned about anything. I shut the bathroom door and began drawing my bath water.

About three minutes later, the bathroom door flew open, and there was Linda, calling me some choice names I can't repeat here.

Mark was aware of Yeager's and my scheme on the bookie raid.

As soon as I had closed the bathroom door to draw my bath water, Linda shot out of bed, down the hall to Mark's room, just frantic. She told Mark I was about to raid the bookies at Tech, would find Mark's name in their records and no telling what would happen. Mark couldn't help but to start laughing and Linda knew she had been had.

We called off the raid for the next morning.

A Mother's Scorn

On another occasion, a group of officers and I did assist an agent with the Federal Bureau of Investigation serve federal search and arrest warrants for gambling.

About 7 P.M. one evening, our agent knocked on the front door of a house in a fairly nice neighborhood of Lubbock. A nice-looking woman, I would guess to be in her early 40s, answered the door. The agent identified himself as an FBI agent and informed the lady he had a search warrant to search the house and premises.

The front door opened into a long hallway leading to the living area of the house. About the time the agent finished his instructions to the lady, a man stuck his head around the corner of the living area, looked down the hall and asked his wife "Who is it, honey?"

"It's the law," the woman said. "I told you if you didn't stop that gambling they were going to get you."

I suspect the husband thought, "Thanks, honey. That comment ought to really help my defense on this case."

Another FBI Raid

After transferring to San Angelo in the Rangers, I was asked to assist the local FBI agents in serving an arrest warrant in the northeast part of Tom Green County. The man we were going after was supposed to be extremely dangerous and the agents had assembled quite a team of local officers to assist in the arrest.

We all met at the San Angelo Police Department about 5 A.M. and were instructed to each bring our rifle or shotgun, plus the body armor we had been issued.

In our briefing instructions we were told how bad this fellow was and then assigned to different tasks during the execution of the warrant. I was to take up a position at the rear of the house with a San Angelo Police detective and cover the back door.

FBI agents were to go through the front door, find and secure the wanted man as quickly as possible, and get him away from the residence as soon as they could.

We got to the ranch property before daybreak and were in place just as it was getting light. Everything started as planned. The agents rushed the front door of the residence and we all expected the shooting to start at any moment. But it didn't.

In a very short while, one of the agents came on the radio and said everything was over and OK and the subject was in custody. We walked around to the front of the house and saw one of the agents standing on the porch talking to the suspect's mother.

As it turned out, the agents had started their entry into the house, and mom, who was up and awake, told the agents her son was in the bedroom in a full body cast—the result of some type of accident.

After agents confirmed such was the case, our suspect suddenly went from a dangerous, get-off-the-street-type individual, to a medical liability for the feds. Standing on the porch, the agent worked out a "PR" bond for our suspect, and we left him in the care of his mom.

Man, That Is a Big One

I have a very dear friend, Glyn Jameson, who I have known for years. Glyn and his brother, Larry Jameson, own two ranches and one of the ranches is located in Tom Green County.

Once my boys got old enough to hunt deer, Glyn let us hunt for many years on his ranches. Mark was about 7 when he killed his first deer on Glyn's ranch.

After Mark got his driver license, we were visiting in San Angelo for the Thanksgiving holidays. I had let Mark drive his International Scout from Lubbock so he and my younger son, Bryan, would have their own vehicle to get around in while we were there for the holidays. On one of those days, Mark and Bryan went deer hunting on Glyn's ranch.

When the boys arrived back to the ranch house that night, Glyn asked if they had seen any deer and Bryan said he had shot a really nice buck and it was on the tailgate of the Scout.

Sure enough, Bryan had killed a big-bodied deer with some wide, thick horns.

At Christmas, we were back in San Angelo for the holidays. Mark had brought his Scout again and on Christmas Eve, Mark, Bryan and their cousin, Jack McCrea, went out to Glyn's to hunt deer.

After dark, Glyn and I were sitting on the tailgate of his pickup and we watched as the boys came out of the river pasture. The headlights on the Scout were on, so we could see them coming from a good distance away. They drove out of the pasture and headed toward the ranch house, then finally pulled up into the driveway of the carport and parked directly behind us.

Mark opened the door on the driver's side and Glyn asked him if they had gotten "another big one." "Yes, we did," Mark answered.

"Really?" Glyn asked. He slid off the tailgate of his pickup and started to the back of the Scout. I don't know why, but I hesitated getting up. I just watched Glyn as he got to the rear of the Scout.

All of a sudden, I swear Glyn jumped three feet straight up in the air, uttering a few words in the process that would not have made the preacher proud.

One of the boys had killed a gigantic rattlesnake and they had it lying across the entire width of the tailgate.

We took a picture of the three boys, standing abreast of each other, holding the snake, its head and tail draping off either side.

Deer killed on Jameson Ranch by Bryan Hunt, Thanksgiving holidays, 1986
L-R: Jarod Jameson, Bryan Hunt

Rattlesnake killed on Jameson Ranch by boys, Christmas holidays, 1986
L-R: Mark Hunt, Jack McCrea, Bryan Hunt

Here, Take Some of this and Settle Your Nerves

One more story about Glyn. In about 1979, the OS Ranch in Post, Texas, hosted a steer roping benefit for the West Texas Boys Ranch. I was a Ranger at the time and had donated my time to help provide security for the event.

Glyn had been on the Board of Directors or performed some type of duty for the WTBR in the past and was at the roping, helping support the benefit, with one of his uncles, Elbert Humble, who lived in Post.

One evening after the benefit had concluded for the day, Glyn and his uncle headed toward Post. Both men happened to have 1979 Ford pickups and, as they got on the road, began to race each other. They raced down the road a ways, and as they topped a hill, they met four Highway Patrol cars. Glyn said he looked down at his speedometer and realized he was going 95 miles per hour.

Both men pulled their pickups over, stopped and waited on one of the patrol cars to get to them. Glyn, being his usual nervous self, got out of his pickup and began pacing back and forth outside the door of his uncle's pickup, kind of muttering in disbelief that he couldn't believe he had been caught racing.

Humble rolled his window down and handed Glyn something. "Here," he said, "chew on this. It will help calm you down." Glyn put it in his mouth and began to chew.

Glyn chewed for a minute, giving the substance time to start working, before he asked his uncle what the stuff was. "I don't really know," Humble replied. "I think it's elk crap. I picked it up in a creek bed in Colorado last month while we were hunting up there."

Make Sure You Have a Good Mechanic

I assisted the Lubbock County Sheriff's Office in many investigations and consequently was in the LCSO's criminal investigation division offices quite a bit while I was stationed in Lubbock as a Texas Ranger.

A young lady who worked in the Lubbock CID office named Karen Conway, and any of us involved with investigations really appreciated her work because she was one of those people who got things done. Besides being very dependable, Karen had a wonderful personality, was very attractive and she knew her business in that office.

One day, Ranger Warren Yeager and I were in Karen's office and she was just bubbling over with excitement about the new car she had just bought. Of course she wanted to show us the car, and we told her we would like to see it. Yeager and I followed her outside to the parking lot to see the car.

It was a very nice looking car. Yeager asked Karen what size motor the car had and Karen responded she did not know, so he asked her if she minded opening the hood so he could look and see what size it was. Karen was sitting in the car and she pulled the hood-release latch.

Yeager opened the hood and immediately pulled the coil wire out of the coil, but Karen didn't see that. She was still sitting in the driver's seat. Yeager told her the motor was a certain size, and asked her to start the car so we could hear it run. Karen turned the key and pressed the gas, but of course nothing happened.

Karen said she hadn't had a moment's problem with the car, that it had always started just fine. Yeager, sounding helpful, advised he did not think the problem was a serious one because the motor was making a sound he had heard many times before. In fact it had a very simple fix. It sounded to him like a stopped-up tailpipe and all she would need to do was run her finger around the inside of the tailpipe to clean it out.

Like always, Karen was dressed very nice and professionally, but she didn't even hesitate when Yeager told her she needed to "ream the tailpipe out." I'll swear, she went to the rear of her car, got down on her hands and knees in her nice work clothes and ran her finger all around the inside of the tail-pipe. While she was doing that, of course, Yeager was putting the coil wire back into the coil.

Karen stood back up and tried the best she could to clean off her black, sooty, finger, and then got back in the car to try and start it. Just as expected, the car started right up, and Karen was really proud she had been able to fix the car herself.

We left without telling Karen about the coil wire, but a day or two later, Karen cornered Yeager in her office and let him know she had found out the truth. She had gone to dinner with her boyfriend the night before and told him about the stopped up tailpipe and how she had fixed it all by herself. She said after her boyfriend stopped laughing, he had told her Yeager had tricked her. There is no such thing as a stopped up tailpipe that can be fixed by cleaning it out with a finger.

It's been more than 20 years since that happened, but I talked to Karen to make sure it was alright to tell this story and we had another good laugh over it. Add "good sport" to the other nice things I said about her.

Don't Leave a Lie Hanging Out There, Number One

I don't remember the date of this little incident, but it had to be the early 1970s.

My partner, Dennis Riley, and I were working days on Highway Patrol in Odessa. Sgt. Brookshire called us on the radio and asked us to go to the regional office in Midland and get two boxes of .38 caliber reload ammunition and bring it to the Odessa office. Each box contained 500 rounds of reload .38 caliber wad-cutter ammunition. We had an area meeting and firearms qualification scheduled for the following day for the entire sergeant area and the ammunition was to be used for the qualifications.

Now, every Highway Patrolman in the State of Texas could recognize these ammunition boxes. At the time, DPS was very frugal with its ammunition and for the qualification tests, the sergeant actually counted out 60 rounds of ammunition for each patrolman to qualify with and no one got any extra. Anyone who wanted to do any shooting off duty had to furnish their own ammunition. Every patrolman I knew coveted the opportunity to get practice ammunition from every source.

We picked up the ammunition and as we were headed back to Odessa, the Midland DPS dispatch radioed us with instructions to go to the French Tool Chrysler dealership in Odessa and pick up the two patrolmen from Alpine. They were leaving their car to be worked on at French Tool, and we were to take them to get a spare patrol car parked at our office.

We met Joe Hicks and Jim Purdue at French Tool as directed. As they put their long guns and briefcases in the trunk, Hicks noticed the two boxes of .38 re-load ammunition and he asked me where I had gotten it.

I told him our sergeant furnished each patrolman in our sergeant area with one box. We were free to practice whenever we wanted, all he asked is that we keep up with the empty brass. I continued that once a patrolman shot all 500 rounds of his ammunition, he simply turned the brass back in to the sergeant and he replaced it with loaded ammunition.

I took Hicks and Purdue to the Odessa office where they got the spare car and returned to Alpine. I never told them any difference on the ammunition.

A day or two later, I was working by myself and I got a call to go to the lieutenant's office in Midland.

"What in the h--- did you tell Joe Hicks about getting practice ammunition?" Lt. Joe Maldenka asked me as soon as I walked into his office. I confessed to what I had said.

The lieutenant kind of laughed and said Hicks was raising holy heck with his sergeant because they were not getting the ammunition deal we were. Lt. Maldenka said he would take care of it, but for me to be careful in the future about "clearing up things" so people would not go off with "incorrect information."

Don't Leave a Lie Hanging Out There, Number Two

I guess I didn't learn my lesson very well with the ammunition-Hicks tale because the devil got hold of me and caused me to tell another not-so-truthful story years later after I was with the Rangers. Again, I can't remember the year, but it was while I was stationed in Lubbock at a three-man Ranger station with Jackie Peoples and Warren Yeager.

One day I got a call from Ranger Wesley Styles, who was stationed in Huntsville. He told me he was conducting an investigation and it looked like the suspect he was after was in Lubbock. Ranger Styles said he planned to travel to Lubbock the following day with a state insurance investigator. They wanted my assistance in getting around Lubbock and possibly finding the suspect. I said sure, I would be expecting them the next day, which I do remember was a Thursday.

About mid to late afternoon on Thursday, Styles arrived at the Lubbock DPS office with the other state investigator, but he said since it was already late in the afternoon and they were tired from traveling, he thought they would just go get a motel room, go eat and rest. They would be ready to start early Friday morning. We finalized our plans, then as Styles was leaving our Ranger office, he asked where Peoples and Yeager were. I told him they were out of the office working, which they were.

Friday morning, Peoples and Yeager and I were at the DPS office. We had our morning coffee, and they left to continue with some cases they were working. I waited on Styles and shortly after Peoples and Yeager left, Styles and the investigator showed up. We had a cup of coffee and Styles asked again where Peoples and Yeager were.

"It's their long weekend off," I replied. "Since there are three of us stationed here, the captain lets us rotate to one Ranger being here on Friday. The other two take the day off and that gives them a long weekend."

Well, I never got around to telling Styles anything different. We went about locating his suspect, took his statement, and Styles and the investigator departed for Huntsville.

Sometime during the next week, I was in my office working on reports and I could hear my captain, Charlie Moore, talking on the telephone to Capt. Dan North in Houston. Capt. Moore said something like, "Dan, I don't know what you are talking about." Then, Capt. Moore began to snicker, his own unique snicker, and he asked in a loud voice if I was back there. I replied I was and he asked me to come into his office.

Captain asked me if I had said anything to Styles last week about us getting long weekends and again, I confessed to what I told Styles. The captain began to really laugh. He got back on the phone with Capt. North and told him Styles had just been "had."

After he hung up the phone, Capt. Moore said Styles was raising some kind of heck with Capt. North because they didn't get long weekends off like we did in Lubbock.

Sisters—What can I Say?

This is a story that will end up about my sister Carolyn, I swear. I just have to lay the groundwork to get us there. And before I even start, let me also explain I did go to Carolyn and ask her about putting the incident in the book. At first she said that I absolutely could not, but she called me later in the day and said if the only way she could get in the book was to have the story told, then go ahead and tell it. One other clarification, Carolyn remembers the incident a little differently than I do, but I'm telling it my way.

The story actually starts with a dear captain I had in the Rangers in Lubbock. Capt. Charlie Moore was one of the best supervisors I ever had. Charlie was of the "Old Ranger" school and left all of the Rangers in Co. "C" free to conduct our investigations as we thought necessary. That way of operation all got changed in the mid-1980s when someone in a union-type job sued their employer for paid overtime. The federal government got involved and forced paid overtime to be paid to most public service employees, and the rest, as they say, is history.

That is a story for another time. Let's get back to Charlie Moore. Charlie loved to have fun and was not above pulling a joke or two on others. He had several little "trinkets" around the office and all of them were used to bring lots of laughs over the years.

One was a little plastic slot machine. Charlie usually kept this out on one of the secretary's desks in the front office. People that would come in the office would usually spot the little slot machine and ask if it worked. The secretary would usually just say, "Try it." The unsuspecting person would pull the handle down, a little clown face would come out of the top of the slot and squirt a little stream of water forward. I have seen more than one man end up with the fly of his pants wet from trying the slot machine.

Another gadget Charlie had was what looked like a small transistor radio with an earplug and cord coming out of the side. On the gadget's front were some key phrases like "naughty talk" or "sex talk." Charlie usually left the gadget on his desk. People would come in to see Charlie—mostly other officers—and when they saw the radio-like-gadget, they would ask Charlie if they could listen to it. Charlie would always answer, "Sure," and hand it to them. Charlie would tell the listener to put the earplug in one ear and press the button on the side of the radio. As soon as the button was pressed, the person holding the gadget would get a low-voltage shock to his hand. That shock scared the tar out of most of them.

Charlie showed up at the office one day with the newest gimmick, just purchased at the gag gift shop in the Lubbock Mall. We called the newly acquired gadget, "Gizmo." Now "Gizmo" was a small rubber bladder-like apparatus, that when squeezed sounded exactly as if someone was passing some serious gas. Well Charlie got laugh after laugh with Gizmo. It was really a favorite laugh-getter.

One day I got to thinking, "Why should Charlie be having all the fun with Gizmo?" I went out to the mall, bought a Gizmo for my own and began having a little fun myself around the area I worked. If fact, I got pretty good at mastering Gizmo.

We went home to San Angelo that year for the holidays, like we usually did. One evening the three brothers, our sister, nieces and nephews were sitting around the big dining room table with Mother, really having a good time. Daddy had already gone to bed.

I don't know how it got there, but all of a sudden, there in my hand was "Gizmo." Seemed like a perfect time for a real sound-off, or at least I thought so. Of course I can't take any of the credit.

I put "Gizmo" between my legs underneath the table and squeezed, but I guess I choked. "Gizmo" and I produced one of our worst sound productions ever. I looked around and no one seemed to have heard anything. I waited a few minutes and ripped another one. This time "Gizmo" performed immaculately. I was right proud to claim this one.

All of a sudden, Carolyn, who was sitting directly across from me, looked at me with this "so what" look. "You are not the only one who can do that," she said proudly. About that time, she lifted up her leg and let one go. I don't think hers was a Gizmo facsimile however.

When I got Carolyn's permission to tell this story she told me one of the funniest things she remembers is that after everyone quit rolling on the floor laughing, my son Mark made the comment that he didn't know "you could just call one up on demand like that."

Happy 50th Birthday

My wife Linda is not an easy person to surprise, and the year she was going to turn 50 years old, I knew it was going to be next to impossible to do a surprise party for her. But as the year wore on and I thought about it, I believe I came up with a plan that totally surprised her.

In the summer of 1996, we bought a ranch in Schleicher County and I am not exaggerating at all when I say we spent many hours working on our ranch, clearing brush, doing fence repair, etc… The work never quit. It was hard work and it left you drained at the end of the day. Several weeks before Linda's actual birthday, we spent an afternoon down at the ranch working as hard as we always did. Of course, that afternoon's work was a specific part of my grand plan. At the time, we lived just outside of San Angelo in a subdivision called Highland Range. To live in Highland Range, residents had to pay a yearly membership fee. In addition to that there was a swimming pool for the members use, but homeowners had to also pay another pool-use fee. The pool was located about a block from where we lived, but not necessarily within our view. Arrangements had been made for "surprise party guests" to park their cars at the swimming pool. From the pool, it was arranged for one or two carriers to "shuttle" people from the swimming pool to our house.

Now I should say, many people, besides me, were involved in planning this little operation. As usual that afternoon Linda and I worked at the ranch until dark and then we headed home. As it happened to turn out that day, we had our oldest granddaughter, Brittny, with us, but Brittny was aware of what was going on. When we turned on Edinburgh, headed toward our house, you could barely make out the swimming pool. Because I was expecting them to be there, I looked, and sure enough, a lot of cars were parked around the pool. As we pulled up in the driveway of the house, it was totally dark inside, just like it was supposed to be. We got out of the car and headed toward the front door. As soon as Linda opened the door and took a step inside, all the lights came on and everyone hollered, "Happy Birthday." It was a total surprise. Linda did not have on any makeup and her hair was matted, she had sweat lines on her face and her clothes were muddy, but she seemed to enjoy the surprise birthday party, even though it was a few weeks away from her actual birthday. I think everyone really enjoyed the evening.

Linda's surprise fiftieth birthday party, San Angelo, TX.
November 1997

The Lighter Side of DPS

Not often does the DPS show lightheartedness, but such was the case in November of 1992. At that time there was a big push not only for Rangers, but all of criminal law enforcement, to file daily activity reports. Now seriously, some things were reported that meant absolutely nothing to anyone and didn't add a thing to the case file but additional paper weight. Such was the situation for the case I was involved with on Nov. 18, 1992. A copy of the offense report I sent to Austin on this investigation is printed at the end of this chapter. The offense title is Questionable Death, Ralls, Crosby County, Smokey D. Bear, 11-18-92. The report (and the title) is self-explanatory, so I will let the reader form his or her own opinion about it. Though I did spend several hours investigating this case, to this day, I cannot believe my report was accepted and actually assigned a Ranger Case Number.

TEXAS DEPARTMENT OF PUBLIC SAFETY
CRIMINAL LAW ENFORCEMENT DIVISION

REPORT OF INVESTIGATION   DATE: 11/20/92

FILE TITLE	
1 QUESTIONABLE DEATH - #0007 2 RALLS, CROSBY COUNTY - #054 3 SMOKEY D. BEAR 4 11-18-92	THIS REPORT IS THE PROPERTY OF TEXAS DPS-CLE DIVISION. NEITHER IT NOR ITS CONTENTS MAY BE DISSEMINATED OUTSIDE THE AGENCY TO WHICH LOANED.

		FILE NR	TYPE	PROGRAM
ACTIVE: ____ CLOSED: X ___		RC092494.	C	1900
RESTRICTED: ____				
STATIONED: LUBBOCK		DISSEMINATION		CX RELATED FILES
SUBMITTING INVESTIGATOR		D1		F1
INV-ID-NR: 1192 BY: J. HUNT		D2		F2
SUP-ID-NR: 1923 BY: C. WEATHERS DATE: 11/24/92		D3		F3
CPT-ID-NR: BY: DATE:		D4		F4
SEC-ID-NR: R317 DATE: 11/23/92		D5		F5

RPT-RE: INVESTIGATION REPORT

SYNOPSIS

Writer was requested by Crosby County SO to assist in identifying bones thought to be human. Bones were identified as those of a bear.

DETAILS

1. On 11-18-92, at approximately 2:10 p.m., writer was contacted by Crosby County SO dispatcher Jane PARKER who requested writer's assistance in Crosbyton. PARKER stated that city workers in Ralls had discovered what was thought to be a human foot and shin bone and Sheriff RILEY was requesting writer meet him in Crosbyton.

2. While en route to Crosbyton, writer was advised by Ms. PARKER on the radio to meet Sheriff RILEY at the Ralls City Office in Ralls instead of coming to Crosbyton.

3. Writer did meet Sheriff RILEY along with Ralls Police Chief L. T. STARKEY at the Police Department in the City Office at Ralls. Chief STARKEY stated that city water meter readers had been reading meters and had found the foot and shin bone hanging from a clothesline in the rear of the residence located at 1013 Main. The workers, in turn, called Chief STARKEY, who went to the residence and cut the foot and shin bone from the clothesline. Chief STARKEY added that the residence belonged to Carlos COLON.

4. Writer viewed foot and shin bone. Most of the meat and tissue had been obviously cut from the shin bone and some tissue was still present in the foot area. The foot did resemble a human foot, but the

CLE-1 (Rev. 6/91)   **DPS SENSITIVE**

Smokey the Bear offense report

CONTINUATION

DATE: 11/20/92   PAGE: 2

FILE TITLE			
1 QUESTIONABLE DEATH - #0007	FILE NO.	TYPE	PROGRAM CODE
2 RALLS, CROSBY COUNTY - #054	RC092494.	C	1900
3 SMOKEY D. BEAR			
4 11-18-92	ACTIVE ____	CLOSED _X_	RESTRICT ____
	BY: J. HUNT		

DETAILS (cont.)

shin bone was approximately 16" in length, which was disproportionate to the foot. Chief STARKEY stated that he had already contacted the anthropology department at Texas Tech University and had made arrangements for them to view foot and shin bone at 4:30 p.m.

5. It was decided before transporting the foot and shin bone to Texas Tech that attempts be made to contact COLON to see if there was an explanation of the foot. It was determined COLON was working as a salesman at Shamrock Chevrolet in Lubbock. Writer requested that Lt. WEATHERS contact COLON at Shamrock Chevrolet to see if he could explain the foot and shin bone.

6. Lt. WEATHERS returned call to writer after interviewing COLON. COLON stated the foot was a bear's foot given to his son by a science teacher at the Ralls Middle School. COLON's son had agreed to bring the foot and shin bone home and attempt to boil same to remove all of the tissue to expose the bones for class study.

7. Chief STARKEY contacted Ralls Public Schools and after talking with teachers confirmed COLON's explanation. This investigation is closed.

CUSTODY OF EVIDENCE

None.

PHYSICAL DESCRIPTION

None.

WITNESSES & INVESTIGATORS

1. Red RILEY, Sheriff
    Crosby County Sheriff's Office
    Crosbyton, TX
    (806) 675-7301

2. Jane PARKER, dispatcher
    Same as #1

3. L. T. STARKEY, Chief
    Ralls Police Department
    Ralls, TX

CLE-2 (Rev. 6/91)   **DPS SENSITIVE**

Smokey the Bear continuation report

Not Going To Smell Good, I Tell You

I have mentioned Ranger Warren Yeager in several stories in this book. Warren has a son named Kyle.

One summer during the late 1980s, we were having a Lubbock Ranger Office get-together at the community center in Shallowater. We were barbecuing hamburgers and had several freezers of homemade ice cream ready for dessert. Warren's in-laws were there playing some really good blue grass music. Everyone was having a great time.

About the time we put the hamburger patties on the grill, I got a call from the office that a sheriff's office in West Texas had recovered a body from the Rio Grande River. The body was being sent to Lubbock for an autopsy and I was asked to meet the ambulance at the Lubbock Health Science Center mortuary and try to fingerprint the body. I told them I could do this.

At that time, Health Science Center had a mortuary in the hospital downtown and a second mortuary in a small building in south Lubbock. Most of the autopsies were done downtown. However, if the body was really badly decomposed, it was sent to the south mortuary. This was done primarily because of the smell or stench that comes from the body when the person has been dead for several days. I was told to meet the ambulance at the south mortuary. OK, that was my first clue things were not going to be good. It didn't matter. I had been to plenty like this before and survived the ordeal. I told the group about my call and that I didn't think it should take me too long to handle the task, but I also said to go ahead and eat without me.

Kyle was about 12 years old at the time and he immediately asked if he could go with me. I told him I didn't think it would be a good idea because it probably was not going to be pleasant. He continued asking to go and I told him to clear it with his dad. If Warren approved of it, I would take him. We would not view or witness the autopsy, just fingerprint the body and be gone. Warren said he thought it would be alright, so Kyle and I headed to the mortuary.

The ambulance was already at the mortuary when we got there and the body had been moved inside. We went in and the attendants were removing the screws from the lid on the casket. These transport caskets have a rubber sealed lid with screws about every 4 inches so the lid can be really tightened and sealed down. Of course the tight seal is needed to contain the smell of the body inside the casket. This was the second clue things were probably not going to be pleasant.

I warned Kyle about the smell that was fixing to follow the removal of the lid and told him he could go back to the car

213

and wait for me. He assured me that he was alright and he could handle any smell there might be.

Well, they finally got all the screws removed and even though the lid had not been raised, you could already smell the stench. I repeated to Kyle that what was about to happen would not be pleasant at all, but he assured me he could handle it.

They removed the lid and the full force of the smell immediately permeated the entire room. Kyle got a good full dose and immediately headed toward the door. That was the last time I saw Kyle at the mortuary. I have to say the body ranked up there with some of the worst I'd ever smelled.

The man had been in the water long enough that his fingers were nothing but bone. I assume the fish had eaten the flesh away. Since there was absolutely nothing to fingerprint or preserve, I was out of there in five minutes. I did rib Kyle just a little over his "ability to stay hitched," but in all fairness, I would not have stayed in that room if I had not absolutely had to.

We got back to the party in time for burgers and ice cream and plenty more blue grass music.

What About That Speed?

In the mid-1980s, Texas Rangers were issued Chevrolet Impalas for their state cars. These Impalas had a two-way display speedometer—one in miles-per-hour and the second one measured kilometers-per-hour. A pushbutton on the dash let the driver switch from one to the other.

One evening, my brother Jerry Don and his family were at our house for a backyard cook-out. We needed some type of supply so I volunteered to go get whatever it was at the store about 4 miles away. Jerry's boy, John Thomas, wanted to go with me. I said, "Sure. Come on." John Thomas was probably 8 to 10 years old at that time.

We got to the store, got our item, and headed back home. It was a farm-to-market road with light traffic and no houses along the way. We got to an intersection with a stop sign for us, about three miles from the house.

As we stopped, I asked John if he had ever gone really fast in a police car. He said he had not, so I asked him if he would like to see how fast we could get up to before getting to the house. He perked up and said, "Sure."

I changed the digital display to kilometers and took off. John did not know any difference. I got up to about 90 miles-per-hour but the speedometer was showing around 140, maybe 145 kilometers-per-hour. John's eyes were as big as coffee cup saucers.

I told Jerry what I had done when we got home, but as far as I know, John Thomas still thinks we were running 140 miles-per-hour.

Ask Your Teacher First

When my brother Skipper's boys were small, I used to have a lot of fun with them. I am not sure their mother approved of some of the things we did, but what the heck. They survived it and are good kids now.

One of the things I remember as a kid is occasionally getting to smoke a pipe or cigarette with some of my uncles or Paw Pa, my dad's dad. This did not happen often and I do remember getting sick a few times.

During my years in the Rangers I smoked small cigarillos (little cigars). From time to time Robert, the older of Skipper's two boys, and Wesley, the younger son, would be visiting over at our house and would want to smoke part of one of my cigarillos.

One of the times we were doing this smoking, the boys each wanted to take a cigarillo home with them. "Well," I said, "I can send a couple of cigarillos home with you, but in no way can you have any matches to light them." Then teasing them some more, I said that the only way they could get them lit once they got home was to take them to school and wait for recess. They absolutely could not show up at school with any matches or lighter, I warned, but I did suggest that when they carried them out to recess, all they had to do was ask the teacher at the playground to light their cigarillos for them.

I don't know if it was Skipper or Cindi who found out about my suggestion, or maybe the boys just chickened out. Anyway, I never heard of them trying to get their cigars lit at school and I am sure I would have if they had.

Taking a "smoke break" with Paw Pa Hunt

Be Sure To Take Care of Your Business

After making Texas Ranger in 1977, I was issued an unmarked police car. The unmarked cars were greatly needed
for the kind of investigative work I would be doing as a
Ranger. Having an unmarked car allowed us to get close to a
lot of things as officers before many people realized we were,
in fact, officers. Now, even though this was the intended
result of having an unmarked car, on a rare occasion it had
other benefits.

Sometime in the early 1980s, I was having some car trouble.
The best I remember, my brakes were not working properly
and my muffler needed some work done on it. I wanted
to get the car into a garage early in the morning so that it
wouldn't be too late in the day when I got it out. There was
a garage not too far from my house in Shallowater going
toward Lubbock. I called Ranger Yeager the night before
and asked him to pick me up at the garage around 7: 30 the
following morning.

The next morning I drove to the garage as planned. When I pulled in, I was the only one there. About five minutes later, a man dressed in the garage uniform came off of the highway and parked on the west side of the building. From where he parked, he could not see me as I got out of my car. I had on plain clothes, but I did have a badge on my shirt and a pistol/ holster on my belt. As the man rounded the garage, he saw me, my badge and my gun, and he immediately started to explain that he was going at noon that day to take care of the traffic tickets he had been issued.

I laughed and told him that all I wanted was to get my brakes and muffler fixed, and I didn't care about any traffic warrants that he might have.

You could see the relief in his face. I had my car fixed and was out of there plenty early that day—maybe even by noon.

The Difference Between Whoa and Go

One day in Lubbock, Ranger Jackie Peoples asked me to assist him and the Lubbock police in serving an arrest/search warrant at the home of Sonja Bush in the southwest part of the city. The plan was to arrest Bush then search the residence for drugs. Bush had a reputation of being violent and had been involved in incidents involving firearms in the past.

The house where Bush was living had been wired for video and audio security. The video monitoring of movements outside fed to receivers located inside the house. In addition to the video equipment, Bush had installed burglar security bars over all the windows and outside doors.

Any vehicles and people approaching the house were easily detected. If Bush or any of her bunch were inside the home monitoring the equipment, it was next to impossible to get near the home undetected.

The first plan to execute this warrant was to gain entry to the residence by driving an Armored Personnel Carrier—or

APC—up and into the front door, but this plan was scrubbed. I don't remember why.

Next, we decided we would use a wrecker to pull a burglar bar off one of the front bedroom windows and enter through the cavity this would leave. There was a small area near that front bedroom that would not be seen by the monitors on the house. The plan was to pull a State Highway Patrol car up in front of the house, but have the Highway Patrolman just sit there in his car. Our hope was the occupants of the house would be "fixed" to the monitor while we pulled the wrecker up to the window, hooked a chain around the burglar bars and pulled the window assembly out of the wall.

The wrecker arrived just north of the Bush residence with a driver and helper as requested. We explained to the driver and helper our plan of action, told them speed was of the essence in this operation, and informed them of Bush's reputation for violence with a firearm. The driver was years older than the helper and he seemed less enthusiastic about this endeavor than the younger helper.

So it was decided the older man would drive the wrecker. He would pull up at the designated time and back the wrecker to a location directly in front of the window. The helper was to wrap a chain and hook around the burglar bars, and then the wrecker was to jerk the window out of its frame.

The wrecker was a standard floor shift transmission and all was going fine with the exception of the driver riding the clutch and lurching forward as he got stopped in front of the window. The helper was working as fast as he could, wrapping the chain around the bars, but he lacked just a few inches of having enough chain to be able to hook the chain hook to the window.

Things were tensing up and the driver made a forward lunge to go. He wanted to get away from that house. Well, when the truck lunged, the helper hollered "Whoa," but the driver thought he said, "Go." That driver gunned the motor on the wrecker. It was just by pure luck the helper was able to secure the hook on the chain and jump out of the way.

The operation worked as planned. The bars and window assembly came out and hit the ground and Jackie and I went through the opening. We actually got Bush and two or three of her cohorts standing at the monitor in the kitchen, still watching the Highway Patrol car parked in front of her house.

We made the arrests and were transporting Bush to the Lubbock County Jail. As it worked out, I was sitting next to her in the backseat and we had gone just a short distance when she looked over at me and my badge. She made some sort of comment along the lines of "What did they send a Texas Ranger out here for?"

I told her I didn't have to be there but I heard the police department was going to search her house and to gain entry, they were going to drive an APC through her front door.

"That I had to see," I said.

Sometimes Looks Will Deceive You

Some years back as I was investigating a murder/suicide case that wasn't going to be too difficult to bring together, I needed to interview several witnesses, who, as it happened, lived in several different counties. I don't think I will ever forget one of the witnesses, a lady who lived in rural Scurry County and who, I might add, was one of the most pleasant ladies I have ever met.

I contacted the lady and set up the appointment for the interview, and she gave me directions to her ranch. She said she was living in the guest house on the ranch. The main ranch house had burned some time back and she hadn't rebuilt it.

I arrived at the ranch and saw, as she said I would, a small guest house located not far from where the main house had stood. The little house was completely surrounded by big trees and there was a fence around the trees and the house.

Now, inside the fence and between the front gate and the door, there were what had to be at least 50 turkeys. I naturally expected them to scatter or fly off when I opened the gate, but all they did was part to give me room as I walked toward the front door. After I got past them, they closed ranks and continued pecking in the thick grass.

After I got into the house, I told the lady I had never witnessed wild turkeys that did not run or fly as you approached them. "Oh that's nothing," she said. "I feed them all the time and when they have picked up all the grain, several of them will come up and peck on my storm door to let me know they are out of food."

About 2 o'clock, I finished our interview and started gathering my things to leave. The lady asked me if I had eaten lunch. "No," I told her. I had not, but I figured I could make it back to Snyder and eat a late lunch there. She asked me if I was hungry and when I admitted that I was a little hungry, she asked me to follow her.

We went out the back door of the house and walked toward what looked like a big, long, two-story barn. We entered, and that's exactly what it was—a barn. It looked like at one time it might have been used to stable horses. The lady started up a set of stairs, and I continued to follow her. Then, she opened a door into a long room that apparently was a dining room. It had a long table with chairs for quite a few people. The lady called out a name, and a man came out of what I guessed was the kitchen area, across from where we were standing. He was dressed in a black, short tuxedo-looking jacket, a white shirt with a tuxedo bow tie and black pants.

The lady asked the man in the tuxedo what had been pre-pared for lunch that day. He told her, soup was on the menu, and though he said what kind of soup, I don't remember what he said. But when the lady asked me if I would care for a bowl, I said, "Sure." The man was instructed to prepare a bowl for me. I sat down at the end of the table, and the man brought me a bowl of soup, along with silverware, a linen napkin and a drink. I was quite impressed. The lady did not join me for the meal, so I was the only one there eating.

I finished my soup, thanked the lady for her hospitality and left. Really it was an amazing experience. I've never had a meal quite like that one.

Vindication: How Sweet It Is

When I was in the Rangers just about everywhere I went, I drove fast. It was just a habit I got into, and honestly, so did most Rangers. I will bet they still do. The Highway Patrol especially resented this and although I don't know of any patrolman who ever took any formal action against a Ranger, plenty of them got upset when they would stop a Ranger, or any other law enforcement officer for that matter.

One time in the late 1980s or early 1990s, I was headed to Austin from Lubbock. I really was in a hurry because I had some evidence that needed to be at the DPS lab—now!

Between Bronte and San Angelo I topped a hill, and, sure enough, there sat Highway Patrolman Roy Blair. Roy turned his red lights on and I stopped. Roy and I had known each other for a long time and as he got out of his car and I got out of mine, he recognized me immediately. He had this disgusted look on his face, even though he didn't say much. As soon as we made eye contact, I apologized for the speed but told him I needed to be in Austin by a certain time. "Well, you ought to make it in plenty of time," he said pretty evenly. Somehow the way he said it made me feel like an egg-sucking dog. After all, Roy had a reputation of a by-the-book patrolman.

I went on my way, but for 15 years, I carried this guilt feeling for speeding through Roy's patrol area.

Then, after I had retired as Tom Green County Sheriff, I was attending a retirement party for Tommy Matthews, a Highway Patrolman who had been stationed in the San Angelo area for years. Tommy and Roy had worked together, and were in the same sergeant area.

At the end of the program when Tommy was speaking, he made a point of going around the room acknowledging some of the people he had worked with over the years. When he got to Roy, he told the crowd how fine a man Roy was, as we all expected he would. But then, Tommy went on to say he had ridden back from Austin once with Roy driving. Until that ride, Tommy said, he did not know it was possible to travel the distance between Austin and San Angelo in such a short time.

All of a sudden, I had no more guilt. It sure sounded to me like Roy could drive a little over the speed limit when he chose to. I asked Roy about Tommy's little comment later that afternoon and all he could do was give me a sheepish grin.

Be Careful Where
You Chain Your Bird Dogs

One year, during bird season, I was working on an investigation involving some stolen farm equipment. We were using the Lubbock DPS helicopter to conduct the search and that morning we were flying over Dickens County, northeast of Lubbock. Pilot Billy Burfeind had come up from Midland to fly the search because the Lubbock pilot was not available to fly.

We had gotten a fairly early start that morning and had been flying the search for a couple of hours. As it was getting close to noon, Burfeind asked me if there was a café in Dickens where we could land and eat. There was a café located on the highway going through Dickens I told him, and I felt like there would be plenty of room to land the helicopter.

Turns out, there was enough room to land. An old abandoned service station was located east of the café and parked between the café and station was a pickup truck with two birddogs chained to the rear bumper.

Burfeind circled the station one complete time, looking for wires or anything that would interfere with a landing, then began to descend for a landing in the area directly behind the old station, coming down from east to west with the direction of the wind.

As we got lower to the ground, one of the bird dogs chained to the pickup bumper came out north to the end of his chain, then turned south and at a dead run broke the chain. That dog continued running south across fields located behind the café.

We landed and I went in and broke the news of the runaway birddog to his owner. He was sitting with several other hunters and they all left to search for the dog. I never knew if they found the dog, though I assume they did.

I told Burfeind later that birddog had probably got up quail that morning for the hunters to shoot and when he saw the helicopter swooping down he must have thought a really big quail was about to get even.

If Only I Could Leave Lubbock

In the fall of 1978, I became involved in what I would call my first major homicide investigation.

An elderly farm couple, Alton and Cora Gandy were found lying beside the driveway of their rural home north of Lorenzo in Crosby County. Both had been made to lie down and were shot execution style in the back of their heads.

At the time, the sheriff of Crosby County was Fred Owen. Fred had been a Highway Patrolman a few years before being appointed to fill an unexpired term as sheriff, so he had only been sheriff for maybe a year and I had been a Texas Ranger just a little more than a year. Neither of us had a lot of experience with this type investigation, but we got started.

The investigation soon centered on Cora Gandy's sister, who lived in Lubbock. Some months prior, the Gandys had signed papers to have the sister committed to the mental ward in Big Spring. Fred and I felt it was a "get even" type murder motive.

According to witnesses, the suspect sister was an alcoholic, and to work that angle of the investigation, it was necessary to interview numerous alcoholics in the Lubbock area. But Fred and I were not making much headway with our interviews. People would just not open up to us.

A patrol deputy working for the Lubbock County Sheriff's office named Sonny Keesee was a recovering alcoholic who had been sober for many years. Well, the thing with Sonny was he knew just about everyone we needed to interview and the people would open up to him.

I went to Lubbock County Sheriff Choc Blanchard, and asked him if we could use Sonny during our investigation. Sheriff Blanchard agreed and Sonny ended up staying with us on the investigation for around a month.

One morning, close to noon, Sonny, Fred and I were interviewing the owner of a small grocery store in south Lubbock. We were all standing outside the store and we could hear a siren coming from the north of us, headed south. In a minute or so, a small van came roaring by followed by a Lubbock city police detective in close pursuit, his lights and siren going.

We jumped into the unmarked car Sonny was using—Fred in the backseat, me in the front passenger seat and Sonny driving and fell in behind the detective. In no time at all, Sonny passed the detective and started closing in on the van. We had no radio communication with the Lubbock PD because they had their own frequencies, but we felt surely the man in the van was wanted for something pretty serious for a detective to be chasing him.

As we got onto the Tahoka Highway, which was two lanes divided, we pulled up beside the van on the driver side. We had our red lights and siren going and Sonny motioned to the driver to pull over. The driver of the van looked at us and started to come over to the inside lane we were in.

We backed off and Sonny then pulled along-side the passenger side of the van. This time Sonny had his .45 semi-automatic pistol out and waved it up in the air so the driver of the van could see it.

The driver of the van again looked at Sonny and began to veer back towards us. When he did that, both Sonny and Fred commenced shooting at the tires on the passenger side of the van.

They were successful in deflating both front and rear tires on the van's passenger side, and finally the man pulled over to the shoulder of the highway and stopped. We had the driver out and handcuffed before the detective caught up with us.

I asked the detective what he was chasing the van for and he said he had run a red light in downtown Lubbock. We got our handcuffs off the suspect and released him to the detective.

Months later, when we had finished our murder investigation, Sonny went back to night patrol duties. And here's another interesting twist to the chase story.

Sonny got a call to go to a trailer park located south of Lubbock for a domestic disturbance. When he arrived at the home, he met a woman who had obviously been beaten. She said her husband had done it and during the interview admitted this was not the first time her husband had physically beaten her.

Sonny asked the woman why she stayed with her husband if he beat her frequently. She replied she had no way to leave. The police had shot the tires off their van south of Lubbock, she said. Sonny did not mention to her he was the one doing the shooting.

Do As I Say, Not As I Do

One more tire shooting story, this time on me, when I was Tom Green County Sheriff.

I was driving into work one morning and was just a few blocks from the sheriff's office. About the time I was approaching a major intersection, the light controlling my direction of traffic turned red and I pulled to a stop, but as I came to a standstill, a speeding car passed me on my left. It entered the intersection and turned left. A male driver was the only occupant of the vehicle, and because he was driving so fast, I immediately thought he was running from the police.

I turned on my red lights and fell in behind the vehicle. We continued northbound on the throughway at a very high speed and as he began to brake to turn right onto another expressway I gained some distance on him. I guess he finally saw me in his mirror. He made his right turn onto the service road of the expressway and continued on just a little ways at a much slower speed. After a few blocks, he turned right onto an intersecting street in north San Angelo, pulled over and stopped.

I did not have my pistol or badge on and was retrieving them from the glove box as the man stepped out of his car. From the way he stood by the driver door, it occurred to me it would be a good idea to get my handcuffs, which were hanging on the turn signal lever of my car. I stuck the pistol and handcuffs in my belt.

I introduced myself as the sheriff of the county and showed the man my badge and ID card. I told him the reason I had stopped him, but now I don't remember if he said anything, agreeable or not, in reply.

I looked into the back seat area of the vehicle and could see numerous items, all new in their boxes or containers. Some of the things were higher priced items, an electric saw, electric drill, small smoking barbecue cooker and there were also fresh meats, beer and other items. The man didn't have receipts for any of the items.

Things just didn't look right to me so I told him I was going to search his person for weapons, then handcuff him for both our safeties while I called a deputy to come help me investigate a little further.

I did pat him down for a weapon and as I reached out to turn him around, he pulled back. To keep him from running, I grabbed the pullover sweater he was wearing. Well, he just pulled down, the sweater slid off of him and I was holding an empty sweater. He ran around to the passenger side of his vehicle, jumped inside and locked all the doors with the automatic door lock. All the windows on his car were up.

He began to slide across the front seat to a position behind the steering wheel. I was standing outside his vehicle by the driver door, locked out.

I had drawn my pistol by this time and as the man put his hands on the steering wheel, I told him if he put the car in gear and tried to take off, I was going to shoot out his tires.

Sure enough, he put the car in gear and began rolling forward and sure enough, I pointed at the front tire and pulled the trigger. CLICK. I had forgotten to jack a live round into the chamber of my pistol as I exited my car. I quickly jacked a live round into the chamber and fired one shot at the front tire. The shot found its mark and the tire deflated almost immediately. I got into my car and began pursuit—at a much slower speed.

I called for help and the San Angelo Police Department and our deputies responded. In a matter of minutes, after a short vehicle and foot chase, the suspect was once again in custody.

Investigation revealed the man had been released from our jail early that morning, had borrowed the car he was driving from a girlfriend and gone on a shoplifting spree. The food items, beer and cooker were all for a cookout celebrating his getting out of jail. The other items were to be pawned or sold for cash.

One of the deputies jokingly told me I might not have followed policy to the letter on my shooting the tire. It was a policy I had implemented when I took office in 2001.

He had a point, but I replied, "Well, as Sheriff I can implement policy and I can suspend policy and that's exactly what I did. At the time I needed to shoot, I suspended the policy on shooting, but after it was over, I re-implemented the policy."

This was one of those incidents that made the rounds. My Chief Deputy, Truman Richey, told someone I was the only lawman he knew of who shot a tire out on a suspect car before the chase began.

But I have to say, there's a follow-up to the story that makes it one of my most memorable arrests. I have been blessed for a while now to be part of the all-volunteer jail ministry program. Through donations from private citizens to the ministry program, we were able to convert an unused cell in the jail to a baptism room. We had a stainless steel tank made to serve as a baptismal well. About once a month, area pastors come in and baptize inmates who request it and there are usually anywhere from six to twelve inmates who make that request. I always tried to be present for the baptism services.

As part of the service, the pastor usually asks each of the inmates if they have anything to say, or perhaps would like to give a short testimony.

On this particular night, we were in the process of going around the room, giving the inmates just a few minutes to speak. I wasn't really looking at the inmates as we did this, but I was listening to what they were saying.

The pastor got to this one inmate and asked him if he had anything he would like to say.

The inmate replied, "Yes, I'm back in jail because I did a very stupid thing. I run from the Sheriff." I looked up and recognized the speaker as the same man who had led me on the chase that morning. The inmate looked directly at me then and added, "And sir, for that I am truly sorry."

Of course I accepted his apology.

Last Chapter, Final Verse

There is no way to finish this book without recounting the blessings in my life, and there have been many.

First of all, I was blessed to have the parents, the sister, and brothers I had. We did not have a lot of luxuries in our childhood years, but we did have the love, guidance and understanding from mother and dad that made those years special. The values and morals Mom and Dad taught all of us kids have stayed with us all of our adult lives.

My next blessing was meeting and marrying my wife of 48 (and counting) years, Linda Goetz. Linda's parents, Emil and Anne Goetz, raised her and her two brothers, Willard and Donnie, in the same light as my brothers, sister and I were raised. In fact, the Goetz and Hunt families lived only about three blocks from each other when we kids were growing up.

Linda has been an exceptional mother for our two sons. She is very stable and I always knew she was in complete control of our home when I was off working somewhere. That gave me some real comfort and allowed me to be as dedicated to my job as I needed to be.

At the reception in our honor when I retired from the Rangers in 1998, I read aloud a letter I'd written, thanking Linda for her love and devotion.

Here's what I read:

> "In 1964, I asked a 16-year-old gal to marry me. About a month after her 17th birthday, we were married in San Angelo. About three months after her 17th birthday, I moved her away from her folks to Devine, Texas, when I started to work for the Parks and Wildlife Department.
>
> "We had both promised her Dad that if he would let us get married, she would finish high school. She honored that promise by graduating in 1966 from Devine High School, in spite of the humiliation she received from the other girls in her class for being a married student.
>
> "She packed up and went with me as I started my career with the DPS in 1967.
>
> "Without complaint, she endured the pain and discomfort of childbirth twice, giving us two fine sons, Mark and Bryan. As I got to go out every day to work on a job that proved to be something different and exciting on a continual basis, she stayed at home and routinely raised our children, getting up early every day to start the same old chores of cook, clean, wash,

provide taxi service, grocery shop and everything else a mother does.

"After the kids were raised, she went along reluctantly with my idea to build a new house, literally, but she worked as hard as any man while we built this house as she knew we were a little short of the required finances to have someone else build it for us. She was also aware of a goal we both shared to one day own some land of our own, and with this goal in mind, she was there helping me when other wives might not have been as understanding.

"From time to time during my career, I have received credit for successful completion of job assignments, investigations and other achievements, so I have had my days of honor. I also know that my wife's daily sacrifices are what made my career possible and I know there has been very little recognition from me to her for her tremendous contributions that helped make my career so enjoyable.

"So today, Linda Goetz Hunt, I want this to be your day of honor. I am the one who is honored to have you as my wife, friend and co-worker. Thirty four years ago we both stood in front of family and friends and exchanged our wedding vows and I would say to you today, in front of this group of family and friends, I have never regretted that day. I love you. I would ask everyone here to please stand and join me in my applause to you on your day. And it is my sincere hope that one of these days you learn the difference between a crescent wrench and water pump pliers."

Joe and Linda Hunt

As a result of Linda's willingness to help, we achieved our goal of buying a ranch in Schleicher County the summer of 1996. We bought the ranch thinking it would be a nice recreation place with a little work involved here and there— mending fences, clearing brush, working cows, etc.

It turns out the ranch has been almost constant work. It has almost killed both Linda and me. And, two of our poodles have been killed by rattlesnake bites there. The ranch is where I had my heart attack in May of 2004, while working on the fences. After almost dying from the heart attack, I spent five weeks in the hospital recovering from that.

Linda was helping me, and our son Mark, work calves in September of 2005, and was attacked and thrown up in the air by a mother cow in the pen. When Linda landed from the fall, her leg was broken in two places and her knee was shattered. She spent six weeks in the hospital recovering from the attack.

But, when we're not patients in the hospital or doctor's office because of the ranch, and when we're not working to fix fences, water gaps, clearing brush or working cows and calves, we do have a little time to enjoy the ranch.

Linda and I also count high among our blessings our two sons, Mark and Bryan. We enjoyed being able to participate in many activities with our boys as they grew up. Neither boy was ever in any trouble that I was aware of and they grew up to be men we are very proud to know.

Both boys married, but unfortunately Bryan and his wife divorced after Brittny was born. Mark is married to Jamilyn Lange Hunt. She is a great mother and we love having her as a daughter-in-law.

The Lord has triple blessed us with three granddaughters. I can in no way describe the joy those three girls have brought me.

Bryan's daughter, Brittny, came to us on April 15, 1993.

Mark's two daughters, Taylor and Rylie, were born on June 18, 2003, and September 24, 2007.

All three girls are special, each in their own way.

I was still working while Brittny was growing up, plus her family lived in Amarillo during her early years so I did not get to do as much with Brittny as I have with Taylor and Rylie.

I have since retired and now I get to spend all the time I want with the granddaughters. One of my very favorite things to do is let Taylor drive our Polaris Ranger 4-wheeler with Rylie sitting in the seat between us. We ride around the ranch, doing whatever. We might stop and look for flint arrowheads, pick wildflowers, watch birds or wild animals. Every once in a while, we might even do a little ranch work.

"The bosses" Taylor Hunt (driving), Rylie Hunt (middle passenger) and me

We leave Mom, Dad, and Granny at home so we don't have to put up with any "don't do that" warnings from them.

I have been blessed with a fantastic career, one that a lot of people dream about. For more than 42 years I was a law enforcement officer in the great State of Texas. I served as a Texas Highway Patrolman, a Texas Ranger and the Tom Green County Sheriff. The days were long and I was often required to be away from home, especially in the early years of Highway Patrol and Rangers. The pay was never much to write home about, and often by month's end we were needing that first-of-the-month payday to get here, but as rewarding as any paycheck was receiving a special "thank you" from a family member of a victim or from the victim himself. Some rewards, it's hard to put a monetary value to.

Now, for the final verse of this book, I want to say the biggest and best blessing I have had in all my life is the heart attack I suffered. As a result of that heart attack, I found that our God in Heaven is real and that knowledge has changed my life tremendously.

Truthfully, prior to my heart attack, I thought I was a good Christian. I now realize I was a "good deed" Christian.

All my life I tried to do what I thought was right—be a good father, do good deeds for others. I went to church at least twice a year, on Christmas and Easter.

The night of my heart attack, I literally died. I was aware I had quit breathing. I remember a very indescribable peace that came over me. I was in a beautiful pale blue setting with a light so bright I could not look directly into it. I remember thinking, "You are dead and this is heaven you are about to enter."

It was unbelievable the outpouring of prayer and support shown my family the whole time of my hospital stay and especially the first day or two. The night of my heart attack the hospital literally opened closed meeting rooms to accommodate those who came to support me and my family.

On the day after my heart attack my friend Glyn Jameson actually plowed his wheat field so the phrase "Pray for Joe Hunt" could be seen by those flying into or leaving Mathis Field, San Angelo's regional airport.

I regained consciousness 13 days after my heart attack and I already knew that when I got out of the hospital, I was to be

"Pray for Joe Hunt" plowed in his wheat field by Glyn Jameson, the day after my heart attack in May 2004

a testament for our Lord, because as I lay there in the hospital, the Lord kept talking to me, telling me I was still here on earth to serve Him. When He spoke, I would tell Linda to "write this down." "This makes no sense," she would say. I told her it would to me in the future.

Several things that happened the evening of my heart attack convinced me it was God's intervention in my life.

First, it was on a Wednesday afternoon and Linda rarely went with me during the week to the ranch. She only went that day to "water her plants."

Secondly, when Linda got me in the car to head toward San Angelo, I made a cell phone call from the front gate of our ranch to the sheriff's office dispatch to request an ambulance meet us on the way. We had never been able to get a cell phone signal from that part of the ranch in the past.

After getting out of the gate and on the highway, I called our dispatch a second time to see if they had called an ambulance. Again, the cell phone worked in an area where we usually had no service.

When we arrived at the hospital and they began to work on me, a renowned heart specialist, Dr. Chip Oswalt, from Seton Heart Hospital in Austin, happened to be there. He assisted in my initial treatment, though to what extent I to this day do not know. Had Dr. Oswalt's schedule worked out as planned, he would have already been on his plane headed home for Austin.

When I finally got out of the hospital, I began to give my testimony in churches in our community and surrounding towns. Each time I was asked to be a guest speaker at a church service, I got excited about being able to give my testimony.

But after giving these testimonies for several months, I began to feel like I was preaching to the choir, and not really reaching that many for God.

Then the Lord came to me and said, "Joe, you are the sheriff and you have a jail full of people who need to know Me."

I asked a few people what they thought of my giving testimonies to inmates and some thought there might be a conflict of interest. But I was sure the Lord had told me that was where I needed to be. I figured He knew what He was doing, so I started giving my testimony in the jail.

At first I would arrange for inmates who wanted to hear the testimony to be brought into the exercise room at the jail and have the guards lock me up with them. This worked well enough until the Lord blessed us with some citizens in the community who donated funds so we could convert an unused cell into a "training room."

I would like to tell of one of these testimonies.

When I first transferred to San Angelo in the Rangers, I worked a murder investigation in which the suspect killed a man in his house and then buried the body on a ranch in a surrounding county.

The body was recovered and the young man pled to criminally negligent homicide and was sent to prison. I remember the young man had a criminal past, and had not had too pleasant of a home life.

Before I gave my testimony, I always liked to go around the room first, introduce myself to the inmate and shake his or her hand. I was doing that one day and one of the men I shook hands with said he recognized me, though he didn't look familiar to me. Turned out, he was the same man I had worked the murder case on years before. He had served his time in prison, been released and was back in jail for some charge.

All the inmates sat down on the floor in the recreation room, and I began to give my testimony. I got to the area of my testimony where I was talking about family, God's love for us and how we all fell short of His glory, yet He would forgive us.

I happened to look down at the man whose path crossed mine years before. Tears were streaming down his face.

I don't know the outcome with the man. I do know the seed was planted. I pray it took and he accepted Christ that day. I did what the Lord had asked me to do and that was to plant the seed.

I'm going to stop with that. I could go on and on, but I think there's been enough storytelling to give you an idea of the blessed life I have had. Anyway, the campfire's down to coals now, and we're out of firewood.

The Greatest Commandment

Matthew 22: 34-40 – "Hearing that Jesus had silenced the Sadducees, the Pharisees got together. One of them, an expert in the law, tested Him with this question: 'Teacher, which is the greatest commandment in the Law?' Jesus replied: 'Love the Lord your God with all your heart and all your soul and with all your mind. This is the first and greatest commandment. And the second is like it: Love your neighbor as yourself. All the Law and the Prophets hang on these two commandments.'"

Credits

Group photograph of Texas Rangers at State Capitol, book cover. Courtesy of Goldbeck Company, San Antonio, TX. lluvia@goldbeckcompany.com   1-800-656-9289

Photograph of Joe Hunt, back cover. Courtesy of David Irvin, The Portrait Photographers, Ft. Worth, TX. photo@dsirvin.com   817-207-9289

Design and creation of book cover, portrait of Linda and me. Courtesy Jim Bean, Professional Photographer, San Angelo, TX. JimBean@JimBean.com   325-653-4187